What people are saying about …

Adulting for Jesus

"This is an amazing book, and will speak to anyone who is trying to find their way in life or anyone who loves such a one. I'm asked to read dozens of books a year for endorsements, and this is the first time I've ever sent one to my twenty-something daughter telling her she has to read it. As you dive in, you will find the same thing I have in sharing the stage with Kristin at many women's conferences: she is both hilariously funny and profoundly insightful."

Shaunti Feldhahn, social researcher, bestselling
author of *For Women Only* and *For Men Only*

"Kristin's hilarious musings and mishaps as a not-yet-arrived young adult and reluctant singleton are in full form here. But it's her honest admission of some very real doubts and struggles that sets this book apart. *Will God really take care of me? If I ever get married, will I still be loved? Shouldn't my life be more exciting than this?* In her angst, she takes us straight to God's Word for answers. If you need new motivation (and legit practical tips) for getting unstuck in a few areas of your life, get this book."

Lisa Anderson, director of Boundless.org,
author of *The Dating Manifesto*

"Funny, inspiring, and all-around amazing! Those are the words Kristin used to describe me when asking that I read her book. Turns out she didn't need to butter me up because the book is awesome. I will never look at Jesus or a burrito the same way."

Bob Smiley, comedian

"As funny on stage as she is off, Kristin Weber offers a delightful and delightfully deep walk through life in her book, *Adulting for Jesus*. On one page I found myself giggling, and on another I found myself gaping at the grace of God, as displayed through the wonderfully creative pen of Kristin Weber. Do any adult (or near-adult) in your life a favor: get them this book, and watch them laugh themselves right into the arms of a loving Savior."

Allison Allen, speaker and author
of *Shine* and *Thirsty for More*

"Kristin Weber is funny and clever in her approach to communication and could get you really excited about pursuing your dreams."

Michael Jr., comedian, author, and creator
of the Funny How Life Works curriculum

"Kristin Weber's new book, *Adulting for Jesus,* made me laugh out loud at times with her witty storytelling and anecdotes. Yet at the same time I was struck at her insight into the issues of our ever-changing culture. She presented the challenges for young adults today as they seek to follow Jesus in a way that has sometimes mystified those of us who haven't walked in their shoes. This book is a must-read for young adults as well as those who seek to encourage and mentor them."

Melissa Spoelstra, author of *The Names of God* and other Bible studies and books

"Kristin Weber is amazing. Not only because she plays the accordion, a skill that she notes has propelled her from rags to nicer rags, but because she is very, very funny. Funny in a vulnerable kind of way that catches you off-guard and opens you up to her practical, wise advice about growing into adulthood. I hope *Adulting for Jesus* becomes a classic for the millennial generation and those who love them and live with them."

Dr. Jeff Myers, president of Summit Ministries

"People ask me to endorse books all the time and normally I think things like *How did Tim Hawkins get my email address?* or *When did he have time to write a book; isn't he running for reelection?* But when I got this book I couldn't put it down, which was awkward because it was on my laptop and a Comadore 64 is very heavy to hold. This book is funny, thought provoking, and will completely change how you look at burritos."

Jonnie W., comedian

"The first time I met Kristin, I walked away thinking, *What a breath of fresh air!* Her writing style matches my in-person experience and offers the perfect mix of both humor and wisdom. You will love this book and feel like you are having a conversation with a long-time friend. If ever there was a time for a dose of Kristin, it is now!"

Vicki Courtney, bestselling author and speaker

"I really enjoyed this book; the grammar was perfect! Also, I am really glad Kristin finally got a job and a plan for her life."

Kerri Pomarolli, comedian, actress, author of *Confessions of the Proverbs 32 Woman*, KerriPom.com

"With passion and depth, Kristin guides readers not only to discover God's will for their lives but to live in the center of it and live joyfully! 'Many of us love rules and formulas (and essential oils) because they give us confidence that things will go a certain way.' It's with this kind of humorous guidance laced with Scripture and depth that Kristin assists young adults in making the most of their lives. This is a must-read for any young adult who wants the most out of life."

Susie Shellenberger, DD, author of 57 books and full-time speaker

"Kristin Weber is an adult who does things for Jesus. She could not be more qualified to write this book. And of the accordion-playing comedian authors I know, she's top 3."

Dustin Nickerson, stand-up comedian (Comedy Central, Netflix)

Adulting

for Jesus

Kristin Weber

Adulting

for Jesus

A BOOK ABOUT PURPOSE,
TRUSTING GOD,
& (OBVIOUSLY) BURRITOS

DAVID **C** COOK™

transforming lives together

ADULTING FOR JESUS
Published by David C Cook
4050 Lee Vance Drive
Colorado Springs, CO 80918 U.S.A.

Integrity Music Limited, a Division of David C Cook
Brighton, East Sussex BN1 2RE, England

The graphic circle C logo is a registered trademark of David C Cook.

Library of Congress Control Number 2020942564
ISBN 978-0-8307-8185-0
eISBN 978-0-8307-8186-7

The Team: Stephanie Bennett, Megan Stengel, Jack Campbell, Susan Murdock
Cover Design: James Hershberger
Cover Images: Getty Images

Printed in the United States of America
First Edition 2021

2 3 4 5 6 7 8 9 10 11

012521-KEP

To my dad and mom, for showing
me Jesus from day one.

Contents

INTRODUCTION

People Tell Me Things

Last year I spent some time with my friend Lisa at her house in Colorado Springs. Lisa and I met working on staff at a summer camp as teenagers, and our friendship has deepened over the years. We get each other, and love spending time together when we can, but Lisa's life couldn't look more different from mine. Lisa got married in her early twenties, and she and her husband live at the base of the Rocky Mountains raising their six (soon to be seven) kids. They've moved only once, a few miles from where they started their life together. Lisa's home is delightfully chaotic, with children going about their homework, chores, and play. I, on the other hand, have moved six (soon to be seven) times as an adult, am still single in my midthirties, and don't have children. I make my living dragging an accordion all over the United States performing goofy parodies for various events, hoping one day Weird Al will take notice and let me open for him. (That last sentence probably explains *why* I'm still single.)

Over lukewarm coffee and with frequent interruptions from tiny humans, Lisa and I talked about life. She told me that despite *knowing* she was abundantly blessed with her life, she felt "stuck." She thought that the ministry she and her husband began together would've brought more stability and financial security by this point and that she'd be more confident as a mom and feel generally further along. Despite our different circumstances, she asked a question I'd been asking myself a lot lately: "Is this how it's always going to be?"

Two summers ago, I taught musical theater workshops at a performing arts camp in the mountains of North Georgia. A beautiful, pristine boarding school served as our "campground" facilities for the week. Unfortunately, the organizers underestimated the number of staff rooms they'd need, so one of the drama teachers and I were assigned (*exiled* might be a better word) to stay in the sick bay of the medical building, which was the only place left with extra beds. Fortunately, my temporary roommate and I got along well and had the chance to get to know each other between our teaching obligations and children coming in and out of the medical center to receive their daily medications. (Don't worry, I didn't administer any medicine ...)

I learned she had just relocated to Atlanta from Hollywood and moved in with her parents. In addition to settling back into her childhood home as a nearly thirty-year-old woman and dealing with the inevitable feelings of failure that accompanied the decision, she was also learning to live with the reality that she might never make it big as an actress. Teaching theater paid the bills, but it wasn't her passion. She told me, "I never thought life was going to turn out this way. And I don't know how to fix it."

I recently spoke with an older woman while waiting to board a flight. She noticed my oddly shaped accordion bag and asked about its contents, which led to me explaining my job.

"What did your parents say when you told them you wanted to be a comedian?" she asked.

"They were actually really supportive," I said. (It always amuses me when people think my parents would be ashamed of my career. It's an uncommon profession, sure, but playing silly songs on the squeeze box is an honorable way to make a living!)

"Well, good for them. My thirty-year-old son just quit his management job to go back to school and study philosophy," she said, shaking her head. "You young people and your dreams. Back in my day, you got a good job and kept it. We did none of the 'bouncing around' you do today."

In the past several(ish) years, it's become trendy to view adulthood as a curse. The other day I wasted a good twenty minutes (okay, fine, probably closer to an hour) scrolling through BuzzFeed listicles about the pains of adulting. Many of the tweets, memes, and gifs accurately captured how I feel as a grown-up. Plus, I appreciated the irony of avoiding adulting by reading articles about avoiding adulting. Granted, these meme compilations weren't meant to be taken seriously, but internet tomfoolery aside, we've all picked up on a profound reality: life as a grown-up is difficult.

If you're reading this book, it probably means you're an adult trying to live in a way that honors God. Or it was the only thing available on the back of someone's toilet—in which case, I'm impressed you opted to do old-fashioned reading rather than peruse Facebook on your phone. I sincerely appreciate that you're giving it a chance. To be perfectly honest, I was hesitant to write it. Writing a book takes a lot of time and effort, and I am only a moderately driven person. Plus, I don't have a rags-to-riches story to inspire you. My story is one of rags-to-slightly-nicer-rags after I paid off my student loans.

I also wondered if I had anything new to add to the conversation about adulting, specifically adulting as a Christian. Many of my observations felt like they might be simple or cliché, and I wondered if the world needed another voice speaking into the noise. A fellow author and speaker, however, offered some advice on my hesitations. She said that the simple truths are the ones we need to hear most often and that God could still use my perspective, humor, and insights to encourage readers, even if those insights weren't particularly earth shattering or ground breaking. She also reminded me that "there is nothing new under the sun" (Ecclesiastes 1:9) and that, at this point in history, all ideas are basically repeated ideas (which was both heartening and sounded like a free pass to plagiarize).*

After adding a joke about writing a humorous book on Christian adulting to my stand-up comedy act, countless people** said they'd buy the book if it ended up getting published. As much as I try to avoid doing work, I'm also a people pleaser at heart. The thought of

---

*   If you're reading this, it means you're allowed to make jokes about plagiarizing in Christian market books!

** Thirteen people, to be exact, *not* including my parents.

letting down my tens of fans drove me to complete the product you now hold in your hands.

In addition to responding to the demands of the masses, I also wrote this book because over and over I've found myself asking things like:

Will life always be this way?

I know I have things "good," so why does life feel so hard?

Did I use up all my chances for happiness and fulfillment?

Why does everyone seem to have this figured out except me?

Sure, I have options, but how do I know which direction to go?

If God's going to make everything new, does what I do now matter in the end anyway? I just have to "tough it out" until heaven, right?

I've learned I'm not the only one asking these kinds of questions. I've had an increasing number of conversations in the past several years with twenty- and thirty-somethings about the fears, expectations, and pressures of adulthood.

Many young adults today feel completely burnt out before they've even landed their first "real" jobs. In the meantime, while trying to figure things out and answer these deep, soul-heavy questions, they're given a lot of flak for living in a state of "extended adolescence." However, it's my humble observation that millennials and younger generations received inconsistent and conflicting messages from those who raised us. A comedian friend of mine pointed out that his elders always told him to "enjoy youth, pursue your dreams, and don't be like us and rush into getting tied down." Now, as he's followed their advice, those same people are quick to say, "Grow up! Your dreams are irresponsible! Be more like we were at your age!" I don't think it's intentional, but the messages preached often have a double standard.

Our culture holds its own unique variety of challenges and obstacles, and just because a trial isn't directly related to physical survival doesn't mean it deserves to be immediately disregarded as petty, stupid, or "snow flaky." Navigating adulthood gets difficult even when there's no imminent threat of a virus, gangrene, or famine. It's true we have more comfort, options, and access to opportunity than ever before, but these advantages seem to shackle us to anxiety, fear, and depression rather than free us to live fuller lives. Perhaps because, once we have them, we realize they don't solve the deepest issues in our hearts. (More on that in chapter 3.)

As Christians, we're frequently challenged by church leaders to find and fulfill unique callings, live with purpose, and dream big dreams that will change the world for God. Often, though, these pursuits don't lead where we expect, or the day-to-day realities of life make chasing our dreams difficult. We wonder if we misheard God about our calling, took the wrong path, or accidentally missed the train leading to our all-fulfilling purpose. The remarkable truth about significance is that most significant actions, in the moment, feel insignificant.

I get it. I am, by mainstream societal standards (and sometimes church standards), a failure. I'm thirty-five years old, have never been married, don't have children, and am not a raging success professionally (until this book gets onto the *New York Times* bestsellers list, of course—thank you in advance for encouraging everyone you make eye contact with to buy it). I possess none of the things we believe we need to be joyful and happy. Yet I find my life today incredibly fulfilling and wouldn't trade it for anything.

My path to contentment and joy wasn't straightforward. I was a directionless college student, changing schools three times and my major four times. I finally graduated with a degree in journalism, which I picked because it required the least amount of math classes. I then became an anxious and aimless twenty-something, jumping around to various jobs, taking comedy and writing classes without clear goals, and searching high and low for my calling and purpose. I desperately wanted to believe I was chosen by God for something special. I saw any success as God's approval and any failure as His tangible disappointment.

Joy and fulfillment came through much fear, heartache, and struggle in my twenties, but I have by no means discovered a holy grail for happiness. My joy and contentment levels aren't constant. I often have to stop and remind myself of my purpose, calm my fears and anxieties about what life will look like tomorrow, and re-examine what gives this seemingly futile life meaning. I've seen God's tender hand and loving mercies as He's shaped me, disciplined me, given me purpose, and moved me toward holiness through this experience we now call "adulting."

Each of us has been granted a set of days to live out for God's glory, and we need to honestly evaluate how we're handling our lives and faith in the day and age we've been placed. You're not a millennial, Gen Zer, or (insert your generation title here) by accident, and you're not failing at life simply because you don't own a house yet but want to find meaning in your work.

My hope is that each person reading this finds contentment in their God-given talents and resources, feels free from the pressure to "have it all," and gets excited about pursuing their dreams. Though it's geared toward those finding their footing in the adult world, this book is really for anyone wondering if they're doing life "right." I hope you find the stories and insights within these pages helpful and encouraging as you seek to honor the Lord in your adulting. (Or at the very least, I hope you find ranting about it on Goodreads therapeutic.)

So without further introduction, we're going to kick things off by looking at an area of our spiritual life that holds a lot of personal interest to every person trying to adult for Jesus ... cue epic page turn (or the moderately less epic tapping of the screen if you're reading this digitally).

CHAPTER 1

Chasing Unicorns, Callings, and Perfect Decisions

"The one aim of the call of God is the satisfaction of God, not a call to do something for Him."
Oswald Chambers, *My Utmost for His Highest*

Last year I performed comedy for a women's conference at a small church in Baltimore, Maryland. After the show, a young woman hovered around my book table, glancing through the pages of the two advice books for teens that I had cowritten while in my twenties. Now that I'm in my thirties, I laugh at myself for thinking I had anything figured out in my twenties. I'm also relatively certain when I hit my forties, I'll look back at *this* book and realize I had no clue about anything. (Feeling confident about your choice of reading material yet?)

"Do you have any advice books for someone in their early twenties?" the young woman asked.

"Not yet," I told her. "But I'm hoping to write one eventually."

"If you do, I'll read it."

We continued chatting, and I learned she was in community college and didn't really have a plan for her life. She explained how all her friends had moved on to bigger universities, gotten married, or reached other exciting milestones, and she was still trying to figure things out. On top of that, her friendships had changed as everyone in her circle had moved into their next life phase; she felt lonely and isolated. Even church was difficult because while people asked *about* her life, they rarely invested in it. They offered vague solutions to her problems while her soul cried out for deeper meaning and connection.

Then she asked a question that I get fairly often at events, but it still always surprises me.

"When did you know that comedy was your calling?" she asked.

"Honestly, I'm still not sure it's my long-term calling," I told her. "I love it and can't believe I get to do it for a living, but I'm not sure I'm meant to do it forever."

"Really?" she asked, a spark of hope in her eye. "That's weirdly encouraging because it feels like everyone except for me has found this big calling and I'm the only one stuck figuring out what I'm supposed to do with my life."

God's Will and Calling

We don't often think about what God is calling us to do in the smaller, ordinary areas of life. For example, I've never once asked God what He was calling me to eat for breakfast. (For all the intermittent fasters, just pretend this whole analogy is about the one meal you *do* eat … which I guess would still technically be breakfast.) I'm hungry in the morning, so I pick something that sounds good. I know I'll get another shot at breakfast in twenty-four hours, and therefore I don't overthink it. I also know choosing something relatively healthy sets me up for a better day, but unless I decide to eat a bowl of glass shards, the immediate consequences of a poor breakfast choice aren't too far reaching. I may feel queasy or lethargic if I consume half a cake and a liter of Mountain Dew, but I know I can redeem myself at the next meal, should I choose to do so. All that to say, I don't spend a ton of time wondering if the heart of God longs for me to eat a bagel or yogurt for breakfast.

In bigger life decisions, however, we tend to do the opposite: we think, rethink, and over-analyze what God might be calling us to do (probably because we know the long-term consequences of picking a career, a spouse, or where to live are much further reaching than simply adding a vegetable to our next meal). While it's wise to approach big decisions with thought and prayer, we sometimes put too much pressure on ourselves to perfectly discern God's calling and make flawless decisions.

In our day and age, we most frequently associate the word *calling* with our occupation. We feel called to medicine or missions or teaching or engineering and devote a lot of time, energy, and resources establishing ourselves in a certain field. We'll talk more specifically about work in chapter 4, but in order to understand and appreciate the purpose of our job-related efforts, we must first understand God's ultimate call to His children: the call to holiness.

The Bible has some pretty specific things to say about this calling:

> He has told you, O man, what is good;
> and what does the LORD require of you

but to do justice, and to love kindness,
    and to walk humbly with your God? (Micah 6:8)

Give thanks in all circumstances; for this is the will of
God in Christ Jesus for you. (1 Thessalonians 5:18)

For this is the will of God, your sanctification.
(1 Thessalonians 4:3)

Do not be conformed to this world, but be trans-
formed by the renewal of your mind, that by testing
you may discern what is the will of God, what is
good and acceptable and perfect. (Romans 12:2)

The will of God isn't meant to be a mystery you have to decode
in order to live a full and purposeful life. Details of His exact plan
for your life remain mysterious simply because He knows the end at
the beginning and you do not. God already knows the future, and
you're still trying to figure out how to squeeze both an oil change and
a dentist appointment into today.

God has always been clear, though, about what He wants from
His children: our devotion. Jesus showed us this in Matthew when
the Pharisees tried to test Him by asking:

"Teacher, which is the greatest commandment in
the Law?"
    Jesus replied: "'Love the Lord your God with all
your heart and with all your soul and with all your

mind.' This is the first and greatest commandment. And the second is like it: 'Love your neighbor as yourself.' All the Law and the Prophets hang on these two commandments." (Matthew 22:36–40 NIV)

To put this in Christian bumper-sticker terms: Love God, Love People.

To put this in Christian bumper-sticker terms: Love God, Love People.

This devotion to God means seeking Him daily and obeying His commands. Keep in mind as we talk about obeying God's law: we don't obey it as a way to earn His favor. We already have God's favor through our faith in Jesus Christ. God's love for His children is unwavering and unmovable. It's our understanding of this love, and of God's gifts of salvation and grace, that should fuel our desire to obey His moral law.

God's command to obedience weaves purpose and mission into every fiber of our day. And because His commands deal directly with the heart and its pull toward sin, they can be lived out in any job, circumstance, or situation. We can do justice, love mercy, give thanks, renew our minds, and walk humbly with God whether we take the job in Colorado or Alabama; whether we spend the morning giving a deposition in court or halving grapes for our toddler's lunch; and whether we're crunching numbers for a Fortune 500 company or cleaning the facilities at a local gym.

More than anything, God's will is for us to grow closer to Jesus and express His love to others. He desires us to be holy, as He is holy (1 Peter 1:16). The other things we view as "callings"—jobs, family, ministry—can be given and taken away. Layoffs happen. Children grow and leave the home. The church we were once called to serve at closes its doors. The call to honor God with our attitude and actions, however, stands until we take our final breaths.

We'll never reach moral perfection this side of heaven, but as we mature spiritually, we'll move further and further in the right direction. As we grow closer to our Father and learn to resist temptation, we'll find ourselves changing subtly and transforming into people who sin less and trust God more. The more we learn about God and see His faithfulness in our lives, the more we'll grow to love His will, even if it's not exactly what we imagined.

Taking the Pressure Off

This view of God's calling removes the pressure to make the "perfect" choice, but it doesn't always feel helpful when we're evaluating options that greatly impact the rest of our lives.

When I was a kid, my siblings and I went through a phase where we played the board game Life almost daily. In case you're not an old-fashioned board gamer, Life is a game where you spin a dial and move your little car piece the appropriate number of squares, with each square representing a milestone that either rewards or takes away money and/or turns. The person with the most Life achievements and money in the end wins. This game definitely planted all the wrong ideas about what makes a life "successful," but we played it because there's something about games involving fake money and tiny cars with holes for tiny peg people that makes children feel authentically grown up.

Anyhow, at a few places in the game, the board presents a fork in the road. You have the option of moving your little car to the right or to the left. Each fork comes with the potential of landing on great squares that could set you up to win, but each fork also comes with the risk of landing on squares that could rob you of your pretend fortune. When we got to those parts of the board, we'd count squares, look at the options, weigh the risks, and then move. Sometimes we'd have to peer-pressure the person stuck at the fork to make a choice and move so the game could keep going.

Like Life the board game, real life comes with numerous forks in the road. Each decision has its own set of potentials and risks. Unlike Life the board game, real life doesn't allow us to put our choices neatly back into a box and stack them in the closet. The stakes are much higher: we must live with the consequences of what we choose.

Often, when we say we want to know God's will, what we *really* desire is a little glimpse into the future to see what joys and trials each path might bring.

We pray for a sign, an indication, or a talking donkey to point us in the "right" direction, thinking the "right" path is the one that includes the fewest hardships. Even though we may *know* God won't forsake us, we often *feel* that God will only show us favor if we perfectly discern His will at each juncture.

Sometimes God supernaturally points us to a particular road, but usually He leaves the decision up to us. Rather than make the wisest decision we can with our limited knowledge, we stress about all our options, wondering which choice will bring us the most satisfaction and the least amount of heartache. We must carefully catch ourselves when we're tempted to think that we can avoid suffering or hardship through our "perfect" choices.

My Story

When I was twenty-one years old, I moved to Los Angeles because I wanted to be a comedy writer. In fact, at the time I would've said I felt *called* to be a comedy writer, even though I didn't know exactly what that might look like. My older sister was moving to Los Angeles and didn't want to go alone, so I relocated with her to try my hand at this haphazard dream.

After almost six years of taking various comedy and writing classes, frequently throwing myself to the comedy club open-mic wolves, dealing with bouts of doubt and depression, and battling thousands of people daily for a single parking spot, I burnt out and started toying with the idea of moving back to my hometown in Texas. I was far from "making it" and felt embarrassed by my lack of success. I wondered why God had given me the dream but not the talent or means to achieve my goals. I fantasized about landing something huge simply so I could leave Hollywood without feeling like a total failure.

I prayed, sought God's will, enlisted the counsel and prayer of my pastors and mentors, journaled, listened, asked again, and still didn't feel confident about what God was calling me to do. Leaving felt like admitting defeat. Staying felt overwhelming and pointless (and expensive).

Advice from my friends, pastors, and mentors ranged from "When it's time to go, you'll just know" to "The enemy wants you to run when God might be asking you to stay and fight." It gave me good things to think about, but no single piece of advice made the decision obvious for me. I desperately wanted to know if staying would eventually bring me the kind of success I craved. I became anxious that I'd regret moving back home. I worried, stressed, and lost sleep thinking about the pros and cons of each option. The only thing I knew clearly was that I wasn't happy with my current circumstances. I needed either to stay in Los Angeles and make some adjustments to my life there—or to take the leap and move back to Texas. (Or I could've embraced a third option: change nothing and accept my misery.) But I needed to choose and move forward.

In the end, I decided to move back to Texas. I continued doing some stand-up comedy from there and taught music lessons, and life during that time was by no means epic. I lived with family to keep my costs down (millennial or not, it's humbling to move back in with your parents after you've experienced adulthood on your own) and focused on using that season to pay off my debt.

During the first couple of years after my move, every time something got hard or went badly, I thought, *Maybe this is God's way of telling me I made the wrong choice. If I'd stayed in Los Angeles, I probably wouldn't be feeling this way.*

We'll only know the ups and downs of the path we decide to take. We'll never know the trials and challenges we'd face on a different road. When things get hard, it's tempting to glamorize the options we passed over. If I'd continued living in Los Angeles, I probably would've said the same thing about my decision to stay.

Instead of spending time and energy "what-iffing" past choices, focus on how God is working in this present moment. If you love God, He has an incredible promise for you that stands no matter what you choose.*

> And we know that in all things God works for the good of those who love him, who have been called according to his purpose. (Romans 8:28 NIV)

God doesn't promise to do what's best for His children *only* if they perfectly discern His will. We can't expect ourselves to choose perfectly because sin doesn't allow our hearts to discern perfectly. The prophet Jeremiah gives us some insight into the condition of our hearts: "The heart is deceitful above all things and beyond cure. Who can understand it?" (Jeremiah 17:9 NIV). If I'm honest, my choice to pursue comedy and writing wasn't purely selfless. I wanted to honor God with my talents, but a large part of me wanted these talents to bring praise, approval, and meaning to my life. Fortunately, God uses us despite our motives, which I learned one summer when I got invited to do comedy in a prison.

---

* I feel like this is implied, but I am clarifying just in case: We must make our decisions within biblical and legal reason. If you go the route of a serial killer, you'll likely (hopefully) live out the rest of your life behind bars. But on the bright side, there's still a chance you'd get to see me do stand-up comedy (keep reading!).

While I was performing at a showcase in Tennessee, the event organizers invited me to join a prison ministry and do a short set in a local facility. I was homeschooled, and prior to this experience the closest I'd come to jail had been participating in a piano competition at a school that had bars on all the windows. Through a logistical mix-up, I ended up performing in front of the male inmates, *in* their living quarters. So in the middle of bunk beds, common area tables, and yes, open showers (where a couple of inmates were, to put it delicately, "cleaning up their act"), I got up to share my wholesome brand of humor. Right out of the gate I made a lame joke about how my parents had homeschooled me to keep me out of jail but they clearly wasted their efforts because I ended up here anyway. One guy laughed.

To this day, that prison set was the most uncomfortable seven hours of my life. (My set was only fifteen minutes, but it felt like seven hours.) After the comedy was over and the worship leader did a few songs, our team had the opportunity to talk with some of the inmates before the guards opened the doors and released us. I was *not* eager to mingle with anyone. I had wanted to leave, get raptured, or tunnel out immediately after my set had ended. As other people from the ministry (who all happened to be guys) dispersed to talk to people, I stood awkwardly near the exit until I heard an energetic, "Hey! Hey! Homeschool!"

Oh yay, I thought. *I have a prison nickname.*

I looked over to see one of the inmates waving me over to his table. Two other men joined him, and I nervously left my vigil by the exit, walked over to the table, and sat down.

"I've got questions for you," he began. "I knew when you said you were homeschooled that God sent you in here to answer my questions because I have been praying for answers and I know home-schoolers know things!"

I was not expecting that. He knew enough about homeschoolers to know that we are (a) usually religious and (b) usually nerds.

He proceeded to ask me some rather deep questions about grace, apologetics, and theology that I (hopefully) answered satisfactorily. It was clear God was working on this man's heart, and because of a bombed joke about homeschooling, I got to play a small part in this working. I saw God use my meager comedic efforts for an eternal purpose.

Part of growing in holiness involves learning how to make God-honoring decisions, trusting that He'll work even our imperfect discernment into His perfect plan. Furthermore, along the way He'll reveal our selfish motives and replace them with true gospel-driven desires.

I don't desire the same things out of my career that I did when I first started. Nowadays I value popularity and top-level success much less than I value the creative process, connecting with people through my comedy, and being able to pay my bills.

When it comes to seeking God's will in our choices, author Sam Allberry puts it this way:

> This is our relationship to God's will: not that he emails a daily briefing of what we're to do each day, but that he gradually renews our minds, changing the way they work, giving us the capacity to discern his will without moment-by-moment direct updates.

This is hugely dignifying. God is not telling us what to think at every moment, but *how* to think. He's rarely telling us what decision to make, but teaching us how to make decisions.[1]

God doesn't give us a highlighted map for our life because if a great big neon arrow pointed us to the next thing, our faith and trust in Him would never grow. Gray areas force us to go directly to God. By putting the choice in our hands, God's extending us the unique invitation to seek His heart and grow deeper in our relationship with Him. He doesn't use us like the little car pieces in the game of Life, hopping us from square to square. Instead, He treats us as sons and daughters, releasing us to cultivate and subdue the world He's given to us.

God doesn't give us a highlighted map for our life because if a great big neon arrow pointed us to the next thing, our faith and trust in Him would never grow.

A few years after leaving Los Angeles and doing the "move of shame" back to my hometown in Texas, a crazy thing happened: I saw blessings from my choices. I completely paid off my student loans and credit cards. Being financially free lifted a huge burden off my shoulders and opened up a whole new world of opportunities. In addition to feeling less financially constrained, some of the work I'd slowly been putting into my comedy career began yielding fruit as well, despite not living in an entertainment hub like LA.

Now that I'm on the other side of that decision, I'm incredibly glad I chose to move back home. I wish I hadn't stressed, lost sleep, or doubted God's goodness. The Lord provided for me even when I was unsure of my direction. Here's the other truth, though: God would've provided for me too if I'd stayed in Los Angeles. He would've provided for me because He loves me and I'm His child. His provision might not have looked like what I *thought* it should look like (fame, fortune, and a white Bengal tiger sanctuary), but He would've been with me every step of my journey.

Your adulting journey will include a variety of struggles, but my hope and prayer is that you'll release yourself from the false burden of making perfect choices and instead see the hope, blessings, and provision of God right where you are.

Considerations

(Use the questions at the end of each chapter for personal reflection, journaling, or in a group study. Or if you're particularly brave, use them as conversation starters at your next holiday family dinner.)

1. What's your understanding of God's calling?

2. How do you see God using your current circumstances to mature you spiritually? In what areas do you think God might be trying to get your attention in order to move you toward growth?

3. How are you at making choices? Are you confident and decisive, or do you stress about making the perfect decision? How can you adjust your approach to choosing a path?

A Little Bit Extra

It's easy to get caught up thinking about the "what-ifs" of another path, but don't let the "what-ifs" of an untaken road rob you from enjoying the "what-is" on your current road. Take a few moments to consider the unique gifts in your life that resulted from your choices.

CHAPTER 2

The Struggle Is Too Real

*"Never throughout history has a man who lived a
life of ease left a name worth remembering."*

Theodore Roosevelt

A couple of summers ago I went to the Museum of the Bible in Washington, DC, with my family. As I explored the various exhibits, I noticed a small book in one of the cases. It was a copy of a German novel released in 1774 called *The Sorrows of Young Werther*, which tells the story about a boy so devastated by unrequited love that he committed suicide. (The book was owned by someone who played a role in biblical education,[1] in case you're wondering how something like that ended up displayed in a museum devoted to the Bible.) The publication became a hit but unfortunately brought with it a string of suicides (allegedly) copying that of the main character. As a result of these copycat suicides, the German government banned it.

The history of the contraband book, especially its connection to suicide, felt strangely familiar to the modern debate sparked over the Netflix show *13 Reasons Why*, which received criticism for over-glamorizing suicide and (allegedly) contributing to an increase in teens ending their own lives. Though, as of now, *13 Reasons Why* hasn't been universally banned, it still struck me how similarly the two scandals unfolded, hundreds of years apart.

"Wow, history really does repeat itself," I muttered to myself.

The author of Ecclesiastes hit the nail on the head when he wrote, "What has been will be again, what has been done will be done again; there is nothing new under the sun" (Ecclesiastes 1:9 NIV).

Right now, younger generations receive a lot of criticism from older generations for being lousy adults. In fact, shortly after I began writing this book, I had lunch with an older colleague who isn't shy about her dislike of millennials. (Many older folks refer to all people under forty as "millennials," but technically millennials are in their midish-twenties to late thirties at the time of this writing. Some of the behaviors people disparage belong to Generation Z, who are currently in high school and college. If you're a Gen Zer reading this, welcome! I plan to take full credit for your responsible adulting.) When she asked me if any new projects were in the works, I cautiously told her I was in the process of writing a book for millennials.

"Are you going to tell them they need to grow up?" she asked pointedly.

"Well, sort of," I said, explaining that I wanted to write a book about the modern challenges of adulting and how to approach them with a godly mind-set.

"So you're just trying to write a book to make millennials feel good about themselves?" she asked, the disapproval clear in her voice. (I suspected she wouldn't be a fan of my new book unless it inspired millennials to publicly and remorsefully purge their luxury apartments of all participation trophies.)

Her perceptions reflect what many seasoned adults believe about this generation: they're lazy, soft, easily offended (we are not!), poor money managers, expect constant praise, and spend too much time on their phones.

"Some of the negative stereotypes may be true, but you know that someone had to raise us, right?" I defended. "We didn't give participation trophies to ourselves."

She looked at me, about to interject, when I quickly added, "Besides, online dating has made us way tougher as a generation than any lack of trophies ever would have."

Bad versus Different

Every generation believes the music, ideologies, politics, choices, and habits of those coming up behind them are dooming civilization. For example, when my uncle brought home a Beatles album as a teenager, my grandmother told him he'd wasted his money on demon music that fueled the band's drug habit. Nowadays the Beatles' music is considered wholesome and timeless.

Humans, especially once they get used to something, tend to resist change. Facebook designers learned this firsthand when, a few years after launching the site, they decided to revise the interface without any warning. This unexpected update resulted in scores of angry social media users demanding Facebook go back to the old design or else they'd cancel their (free, non-obligatory) accounts.*

---

* It seems Facebook learned from that backlash. Recently I received a notice from the social media hub that a new interface is coming (they're calling it a new "experience"), but before the design is forced on people, they're giving everyone an opportunity to familiarize themselves with it and mentally prepare for this life-altering adjustment.

Once we get into a comfort zone, what's familiar becomes what's "right," and the line between a change being *different* and a change being *bad* gets blurred. Sure, people in our generation aren't buying diamonds, china sets, and boxed cereal with the same fervency as our grandparents, but those aren't necessarily bad changes; they're just different. On the other hand, we're accumulating more debt, consuming massive quantities of entertainment, and reporting higher levels of mental illness and loneliness, all of which are undoubtably negative changes. While we generally don't have to worry about the bubonic plague wiping out half the population each year, we still have struggles.**

Issues like anger, lust, greed, laziness, fear, idolatry, doubt, and anxiety have plagued the human heart since Adam and Eve first rebelled. The context for exposing these sins, however, varies from age to age. Many of the problems affecting us today relate directly to the material wealth and technological advancement we've inherited as a culture.

As a generation, we've been on the receiving end of numerous blessings. I, for one, am grateful to live in an era of Chipotle and air-conditioning, and I'm glad I don't have to worry about losing a hand due to a paper cut developing gangrene. It's always important to keep an attitude of thankfulness for what's been handed down to us, and to understand and appreciate the sacrifices made by previous generations that led to the comfort and prosperity we benefit from

---

** When I began writing this book, the statement "We don't have to worry about a plague" was true. As I do my final edits, though, most of the country is locked down due to the coronavirus pandemic, so even our first-world prosperity hasn't made us immune to all plagues. For more on this, see the author note at the end.

today. However, gratefulness for what's been given doesn't mean blindly ignoring the issues immediately at hand. God cares deeply and intimately about every generation's struggles. They're not a surprise to Him, and they're not outside His reach of grace.

Rather than solve all our physical problems, prosperity and technological advancement have uniquely revealed our "heart" problems. At first glance, many of the issues afflicting us seem innocuous, even silly, but the ever-present realities of *comfort addiction*, *instant gratification*, *distractions*, and *endless options* can subtly influence our hearts, holding us back from living lives of joy, contentment, sacrifice, and purpose. Though this list isn't exhaustive, most of the issues addressed throughout the rest of the book can be traced back to one of these four things.

Rather than solve all our physical problems, prosperity and technological advancement have uniquely revealed our "heart" problems.

Comfort Addiction

A couple of months ago, I became an aunt for the first time when my younger sister gave birth to my niece. As I looked for gifts and necessities to help my sister with her new baby, I came across a product called "wipe warmers." With a click of a button, my niece would never have to experience a cold bum during diaper changes. But (butt?) what happens when she gets older and realizes that booties get cold sometimes? Would I be contributing to her becoming more of a snowflake if I removed one more discomfort from her tiny little life?

Right now, it is so, so, so, so easy to be comfortable. We have a product for every problem, a drug for every ailment, a device to combat even the slightest feelings of boredom, and an empowering meme for every negative feeling.

We are, in short, a society of comfort gluttons. Most of us feel entitled to comfort, and the instant discomfort sets in we start complaining. While former generations worked *toward* comfort, most of us were born into it. In fact, it's estimated that even a low-income family in America has more comforts than a seventeenth-century king.[2]

And let's be honest, who would pick discomfort over comfort? Being uncomfortable is, well, uncomfortable!

The desire to be comfortable isn't always sinful. Obedience to God, however, often comes with a degree of physical and/or mental discomfort. So when comfort becomes the end goal we're living for, we miss out on opportunities to serve God and see Him move.

We don't have to live like medieval monks, but we need to keep in mind that a lot of our motivation lies in the shadow of what makes us comfortable and that culture and society have made it incredibly simple for us to settle for an easy, comfy life.

Instant Gratification

When I was a kid, my dad let my older sister and me watch *The X-Files*, a show about a pair of FBI agents tasked with investigating paranormal activity. You might've heard of it, either from its original run or the more recent continuation of the series. This show was a rite of passage for me because it was the first "real" show I was allowed to watch, since my dad carefully monitored our TV intake. We couldn't watch *The Smurfs* or *Barney* because of their communistic undertones,*** but he decided that a show about aliens and monsters was okay since they were the aliens and monsters of a free, capitalist society.

The X-Files had already been on television several seasons by the time my parents decided we could watch it. My older sister and I desperately wanted to watch the episodes we'd missed, but unfortunately, this was the '90s and on-demand wasn't a thing yet. Depending on when you were born, you may also remember the dark and savage days before Netflix and binge watching. Unless a network ran a series marathon, we had to perfectly execute a sequence of steps in order to binge watch a show. First, my sister and I had to pool our money to buy a *TV Guide* at the grocery store. Then, we had to go through the *TV Guide* and highlight every upcoming rerun. Next, we had to find empty VHS tapes and set the VCR to record the older episodes. Finally, we had to write notes threatening mortal peril to anyone

---

*** I get the Smurfs, but I'm still trying to get a good explanation of how Barney promoted the ideals of Stalin. I think the overly peppy songs just annoyed him.

who messed with the VCR while the show recorded. After several weeks of vigilant recording, we'd have enough episodes to meet the minimum requirements for binge watching.

We're an increasingly on-demand culture. We don't have to wait for food, water, information, or entertainment. Largely because of technology, patience isn't a requirement in many areas of life anymore. Nowadays, if I discover a new show and want to catch up, with a few clicks of the mouse and a modest charge to my credit card, I can watch all its prior episodes without ever leaving my couch. I can even have binge-worthy snacks delivered right to my doorstep within the hour.

Because we're so instantly gratified in the smaller areas of life, we lose perspective on the bigger-picture things that aren't meant to happen overnight. We get frustrated and anxious if we don't feel like we're making a difference with our lives right away, but many things that matter like love, impact, fulfillment, and joy require an incredible amount of hard work and patience.[3] It's harder to keep perspective on the long-term aspects of life when everything else happens so quickly.

In many areas of life, fulfillment takes time, energy, and a dreadful amount of resilience and perseverance. God often operates outside the immediate and works wonders in our waiting; but because of our instant-gratification culture, we're losing the ability to wait.

Distractions

Today, distractions everywhere pull for little pieces of our attention. On my phone alone, I have (at least) fifty apps attempting to sidetrack me every time I unlock it. If I click into my web browser, the number of potential distractions grows exponentially.

Distractions have created an environment where we're constantly doing something but never actually accomplishing anything. Multitasking gives the illusion of efficiency, but it really just leaves us feeling overwhelmed, tired, and dissatisfied with our lack of productivity.[4]

Staying focused when entertainment, information, and communication continuously rest at our fingertips takes a lot of mental energy and willpower, which can leave us drained at the end of the day. In order to combat the wearing grip of distraction, we have to develop and maintain habits that help keep us on course.

Endless Options

Options are generally a sign of wealth and success, but studies have shown that at a certain point, "choice overload" becomes a source of stress.[5] If you don't believe me, just try to order quickly off a Cheesecake Factory menu. It's overwhelming. Rather than making us happy about a broader selection of options, too many choices cause us to wonder whether we picked "right."

Many of the decisions we must make in life have much higher stakes than choosing an entree off a menu. In dating, occupations, and even picking where to live and go to church, we're often hesitant to commit because we're afraid we'll miss out on something even better.

We have only a limited number of hours in the day and a finite number of days in our lives here on earth. Many of us waste precious time stressing about our options instead of enjoying and investing in what's already in front of us.

So What Now?

We tend to have three responses when dealing with the core struggles of our generation. The first is blaming the people who raised us for our struggles and holding a grudge toward them for not preparing us better for life. Parents are easy targets, but just as millennials are doing their best with what they've been given, most of them raised their kids the best they knew how with the knowledge and resources they had. My parents certainly didn't set out to make adulthood difficult for me. How could they know that the very thing they worked so hard for me to have—a safe, comfortable, trial-free childhood—was the very thing I'd have to "get over" as an adult? If there are gaps in our adulting skills, rather than pointing fingers, let's give some grace to the generation that raised us and get to work filling in the gaps. No upbringing is perfect enough to completely safeguard someone against struggle. Plus, you're going to want that same grace extended to you if or when you become a parent.

The second response involves glorifying the past and wishing for the return of the "good ol' days" of human behavior. It's tempting to put the past on a pedestal, but no generation was, or ever will be, perfect. Sometimes I get discouraged about the state of humanity when I watch the news or hop on Facebook and see long threads of hostile, angry arguments, sometimes over something as silly as a goat meme. I long for simpler days when people sat in porch rocking chairs and chatted for hours over a pitcher of freshly made lemonade, but then I remember that in those days people often fought to the death in duels when they disagreed over something.

We must learn from our past and prepare as best as we can for the future, but if we dwell too much on either, we'll miss the only place where we can actually do good: the present.

The third and most helpful response recognizes and accepts our generation's struggles and sees them as opportunities for personal and spiritual growth. God placed you and me (my mother will read that last sentence out loud to make sure it's not supposed to be "you and I") in *this* century and in *this* generation to live, minister to others, and honor Him *now*. We must learn from our past and prepare as best as we can for the future, but if we dwell too much on either, we'll miss the only place where we can actually do good: the present.

In order to truly wage war on the four "demons" of our age, we have to understand something even deeper about our hearts: the longing for complete fulfillment. But that is a topic for another chapter (the next one, in fact).

Considerations

1. What are some of the criticisms you've heard about your generation? Are they accurate?

2. Which of the four pressing issues (comfort addiction, instant gratification, distractions, and endless options) of today's culture challenges you most in your daily life? Would you add anything to the list of challenges facing culture today?

3. Why do you think people equate "what's familiar" with "what's right"?

A Little Bit Extra

Right now, millennials are in their "prime," but we won't always be the ones driving culture. Eventually, we'll get set in our ways (or lack of ways), Taylor Swift will start performing in casinos, and avocado toast will be relegated to the blue plate special. Another generation will take center stage. Realizing that every generation struggles differently will give us grace and compassion for those behind us. We probably won't completely understand the issues and mind-sets of our children and grandchildren. Instead of criticizing, patronizing, and griping at the quirks of "young people," one of my great hopes is that we'll offer ourselves as mentors, encouragers, and prayer warriors to them. Are we going to complain, mock, and belittle as things change simply because they're outside our comfort zone? Or are we going to listen, encourage, and stand alongside those coming up and help them figure out how to glorify God amid their own set of challenges?

CHAPTER 3

Fading Glory

*"If we find ourselves with a desire that nothing in this world can satisfy,
the most probable explanation is that we were made for another world."*
C. S. Lewis, *Mere Christianity*

I'm not a naturally athletic person. (If you want proof, you can go to YouTube and look up "Why Kristin isn't a gymnast," a video montage my older sister thoughtfully put together about my short-lived childhood gymnastics career.) I enjoy being active, but I'm not terribly driven to push my body to its physical limits. I generally do the minimum amount of exercise the surgeon general recommends and call it a day.

When I turned twenty-five, however, I decided to train for a marathon. Why, you might ask, would someone who is mostly indifferent to exercise sign up to run (i.e., walk and jog) for eight straight hours? The answer is simple: because I wanted to be able to bring up in casual conversation that I had run a marathon. I wish the reason were deeper than that, but I didn't yet have the depth of character I do now. (I also learned too late that, unless you're around runners, one's marathon experience doesn't come up all that often in casual conversation.)

I trained with a local running group for nearly a year before the big race. On marathon day, excitement and electrolyte powder filled the air as I approached the starting line with 30,000 other athletes who shared my goal of running 26.2 miles without dying. My family had flown in to cheer me on. My race bib and overpriced Asics made me feel like Usain Bolt. I was mere hours away from bragging rights, a shiny boomer-approved participant's medal, and some delicious post-race snacks.

While it would take a pretty hefty bribe to convince me to run another marathon, I was surprised by the disappointment I felt upon completing my goal. In the days following the race, I experienced a sort of melancholy letdown. I hung up my medal, finished my stash of recovery snacks, and took several Epsom salt baths, but life seemed a little lackluster despite my big accomplishment.

If you're over the age of six, you've probably encountered the "now what?" feeling that hits at the conclusion of a holiday, milestone, or highly anticipated experience. Our family video camera caught the perfect "now what?" moment one year when the month(s)-long buildup to Christmas ended with my brother cynically asking after ripping open his last present, "Is that all there is?"

I've often wondered what drives gold-medal athletes to return to the Olympics after they've proven themselves as the best in the world. Or why actors and actresses on acclaimed television shows feel the need to try to break into movies. Or why we lose our minds and scramble to immediately get the newest iPhone, even though the former model still far exceeds what we'd ever need from a personal, pocket-sized computer. Why do we grow bored and dissatisfied with what we already have?

The problem is this: glory fades. That medal, new job, or fresh-off-the-assembly-line gadget *can* fill you up, but only for a while. Other people's achievements soon overshadow your own accomplishments. The excitement of a new job wilts into the daily monotony of showing up and putting out the same fires. New gadgets begin getting old the instant they're off the assembly line. Still, despite this reality, we continue our quest to "have it all." We look for bigger, bolder, and shinier ways to bring back sensations of excitement, anticipation, and fulfillment. We think the *next* job, the *next* relationship, the *next* goal reached will be the thing that brings us the permanent fulfillment we crave.

Even "spiritual highs" fade. During the summers of my late teens and early twenties, I attended and then worked at a Christian camp in the mountains of Colorado. The tight-knit community, frequent robust discussions about life and theology, and stunning mountain scenery filled me up so completely that I'd return home feeling ready to handle anything life threw at me. (Now that I think about it, I'm pretty certain this feeling is referred to as a "camp high.") It wouldn't take long, though, before I'd start getting anxious and stressed again about the pressures of life, even though mere weeks prior I'd literally and figuratively been on top of a mountain.

One of the more sobering realities of life is that excitement often gives way to the mundane, and the things that fill you today may leave you empty tomorrow. In fact, it seems like the greater the excitement, the bigger the letdown, and the higher you go, the further you have to fall.

I know that sounds a little depressing, but please stay with me. If we're going to "adult" effectively for Jesus, it's important that we understand the spiritual reality of *why* we continually get caught in a cycle of seeking fulfillment from earthly experiences and material possessions, and why, even after we've surrendered our lives to God, we still sometimes feel emptiness and longing. To understand this *why*, we need to go all the way back to the Old Testament.

If we're going to "adult" effectively for Jesus, it's important that we understand the spiritual reality of why, even after we've surrendered our lives to God, we still sometimes feel emptiness and longing.

Understanding Why

In the book of Exodus, we're told an interesting story about Moses. (Note: The following section would be best illustrated by using a felt board and Bible-character cutouts. But since this is a book and not a '90s-era Sunday school classroom, I'll do my best to explain my points with boring old words.) After leading God's people out of slavery in Egypt, Moses went up Mount Sinai to talk to God on behalf of the people. When Moses returned, his face was physically shining from being in the presence of the Lord (Exodus 34:29–32).

At the church I attend currently, the pastor always concludes with a benediction that uses the phrase "May the Lord make His face shine upon you." When the Lord's face shines upon us—when His presence has been overwhelmingly felt—our countenance changes. Moses, who actually sat in the physical presence of God, absorbed God's glory and literally glowed. However in the next few verses, we're told that Moses put a veil over his face to hide the shine from his fellow Israelites (Exodus 34:33–35). We're not given much of a reason as to why Moses did this until the New Testament, when the apostle Paul finally explained this seemingly strange behavior.

> We are not like Moses, who would put a veil over
> his face to prevent the Israelites from seeing the end
> of what was passing away. (2 Corinthians 3:13 NIV)

Moses didn't cover up his face because walking around like a human Lite-Brite made people uncomfortable; he didn't want them to see the light of God's glory fading.

God's glory didn't always fade, though. In the beginning, when God created the world and mankind, He dwelled *in* creation *with* those made in His image.[1] He called everything He created "good." Sin hadn't put up a divider between humans and their Creator yet, so Adam and Eve experienced God's uninterrupted glory. Because of this, work and play were wholly and completely fulfilling. When

Adam and Eve disobeyed, humanity became separated from God. We could no longer dwell constantly with our heavenly Father, and as a result, the glory of every experience has a shelf life.

Fortunately, God didn't leave us to wallow in our sinful condition with no hope. He provided a Savior in His Son, Jesus Christ. Jesus not only perfectly kept all of God's law, but He took the punishment we deserved for breaking the law. Finally, after being crucified, Jesus conquered death by rising from the grave, providing a way for us to be reconciled *back* to God. Those who repent of their sins and put their faith in Jesus will spend eternity in a new heaven and a new earth, where humanity will be once again restored into the full and uninterrupted presence of God. (This is the gospel in a nutshell.)

Here's the hard part: though the final victory has been won through Jesus' life, death, and resurrection, we still have battles to get through before reaching the end. I've heard pastors call this tension "the already, not yet." (In my opinion, *The Already, Not Yet* sounds like a Christian version of *Stranger Things*. Someone should see if the Kendrick Brothers might want to produce that.) This is why sometimes we feel hopeless about life even after we've been saved.*
Though you're restored to right standing before the Father when you

---

*   I'll talk periodically about depression and anxiety, addressing these two feelings in the context of struggles common to life and culture. Sin has broken everything, including hearts, bodies, and minds. While some depression and anxiety can be managed by perspective and lifestyle changes, a lot of it cannot. Genetics, trauma, and other factors can create the need for professional intervention. You can't "pull yourself up by your bootstraps" if you don't have boots. You may need someone to help fit you with a set of mental boots before you can start pulling yourself up with good advice and determination. If that's you, I hope you find this book a useful resource, but don't be afraid or ashamed to seek professional help.

put your faith in Jesus, your *feelings* aren't going to stay consistent throughout the ups and downs of life because sin and brokenness still litter the world.

Feelings are fickle little creatures. They fluctuate depending on the amount of sleep we've had, our hunger level, hormones, and countless other external factors. Our current earthly vessels grow old, get tired, have chemical imbalances, and fail us. We feel restless and gripped with an internal longing that doesn't make sense, especially if we have a "good" life.

I once heard someone say, "Feelings are real, but they aren't reality." Though our feelings may change, God's truth doesn't. When our feelings fail us (and they will), we must know and be grounded in enough truth so our minds can speak reality to our hearts when our emotions guide us astray.

When our feelings fail us (and they will), we must know and be grounded in enough truth so our minds can speak reality to our hearts.

Having It All

Even if we get everything we dream of this side of heaven, we'll still sometimes feel the inward groaning for something more than the lives we're living. As actor, comedian, and accidental-theologian Jim Carrey once said, "I think everybody should get rich and famous and do everything they ever dreamed of so they can see it's not the answer."[2]

Many of us feel a heavy pull to "have it all," and there's nothing wrong with that if "it" is the right thing. We desire to "have it all" because we're *meant* to "have it all." "Having it all," however, starts with perfect fellowship with God, and that won't be restored until He makes all things new. Then, we'll have all of eternity to "have it all."

For those who don't know Christ, the constant pursuit of fulfillment can be an unbearable curse. If you're in Christ, though, this feeling of longing isn't your enemy. For Christians, this yearning gently points our focus toward the finish line, where an eternity of fulfillment in the presence of our Savior awaits us. (And I have no way to prove this, but I think heaven will include an eternity of twenty-four-hour access to Chipotle.)

This future hope doesn't instantly solve all our current problems, but if we practice remembering *why* we're prone to feeling this longing, we can step in and speak truth to our hearts when our circumstances aren't fulfilling. As we recognize and submit these feelings to God, their grip on us loosens. They may always pop up, but like weeds in a garden, we'll learn to identify lies and pull them before they take root. Gradually, as the lies are removed at their roots, the truth takes hold, allowing joy, trust, and hope to blossom.

The end of our story is magnificent—so magnificent, in fact, that the Bible says no one can even imagine what God has prepared for those who love Him (1 Corinthians 2:9). A day is coming when we'll never feel empty or unfulfilled again. The new heaven and new earth will arrive in the blink of an eye.

> Then I saw "a new heaven and a new earth," for the first heaven and the first earth had passed away, and there was no longer any sea. I saw the Holy City, the new Jerusalem, coming down out of heaven from God, prepared as a bride beautifully dressed for her husband. And I heard a loud voice from the throne saying, "Look! God's dwelling place is now among the people, and he will dwell with them. They will be his people, and God himself will be with them and be their God. 'He will wipe every tear from their eyes. There will be no more death' or mourning or crying or pain, for the old order of things has passed away."
>
> He who was seated on the throne said, "I am making everything new!" Then he said, "Write this down, for these words are trustworthy and true." (Revelation 21:1–5 NIV)

One of the things I love most about following Jesus is that He hasn't left me wondering about my future. I know how my story ends. It ends with me and my brothers and sisters in Christ dwelling in perfect satisfaction with our Creator, in a glory that will never fade.

Remembering our true ending and understanding our longing for fulfillment help establish a framework for the rest of our adulting.

Considerations

1. When have you experienced the emptiness that comes with the end of something? How did you handle that feeling?

2. How often do you think about heaven and your eternal future? In what ways does the promise of eternity encourage you?

3. Does knowing that your internal longing is meant to point you toward Jesus and the promise of eternal fulfillment change your view on the emptiness you feel today? Why, or why not?

A Little Bit Extra

Recently at a conference, I heard speaker Paul David Tripp explain that we suffer from "eternity amnesia."[3] When we lose sight of our purpose and God's eternal promise, we're more likely to give in to negative behaviors without realizing the implications have eternal consequences.

CHAPTER 4

Work: It Does a Soul Good

"Work is a blessing. God has so arranged the world that work is necessary, and He gives us hands and strength to do it."
Elisabeth Elliot, *Discipline: The Glad Surrender*

Growing up I observed two different views on work.

On one hand, the topic of work seemed to start most conversations in the adult world, and many of my favorite shows revolved around the characters' jobs. Even as a kid I believed that my career choice would be fundamental to my value as a person, and I knew I wanted my work to matter.

On the other hand, most of the adults I knew in real life were counting down to their next vacation, or the ultimate dream: retirement. The grown-ups closest to me viewed work as a responsibility and a means to an end, with the "end" being the ability to provide comfortable lives for them and their families. If you enjoyed your work, wonderful! If you hated your work, too bad! Work was work, and that was that.

My parents and their peers were raised by those coming out of World War II and the Great Depression. They were brought up by men and women who were, by and large, shaped by struggle and sacrifice. My grandparents knew the value of hard work and saw many of their problems solved by having a good job. Passion, dreams, and fulfillment didn't matter as much as being able to put a roof over your head and food on the table. Financial security was the dream, not enjoyment.

Views on work have shifted in recent decades, and we're now living in what I affectionately call the "dream big" era. The high value placed on pursuing security and material wealth has given way to pursuing passion, dreams, and fulfillment through our careers.

There are both good sides and bad sides to this mind-set change, and as with many opposite viewpoints, the solution probably lies somewhere in the middle.

Work and the Heart of God

When many of us think of a perfect world, we almost always imagine a scenario where work is nonexistent. In reality, humans actually thrive *more* when they're engaged in some sort of work, and studies have even shown the likelihood of depression increasing after retirement.[1] A friend's mom recently told me about a man in her senior living community who retired a multi-millionaire but became so bored in retirement that he got a job cashiering at a local grocery store.

"Does he like it?" I asked.

"He *loves* it!" she responded.

Work is often viewed as the enemy to happiness, but it's actually a vital part of God's plan.

When God created the heavens and the earth, He also created the concept of work. He made something out of nothing (He worked!); then He put mankind in charge of His creation (Genesis 1–2). Work, at its core, is a *good* thing.

---

*God created work to move us **toward** something much bigger than ourselves.*

Furthermore, work was *meant* to be meaningful and rewarding. God created work to move us *toward* something much bigger than ourselves. Purposeful, God-honoring work brings life, order, beauty, and value to our home, community, and world.

In the previous chapter, we touched briefly on what life before sin looked like. We know that Adam and Eve worked in the Garden, even before the fall. God put them in charge of filling the earth, subduing it, and ruling over creation (Genesis 1:28). This simple mandate included all kinds of work. They had to organize, manage, create, interact, observe, experiment, labor physically, and more as they cultivated the raw materials of creation into order, sophistication, and beauty. Because man's rebellion hadn't broken creation, their work prospered.

And then, sin fractured everything, including the harmony of work. Work wasn't part of the curse; work *became* cursed because of sin. Instead of working *with* humanity, creation now worked *against* humanity. Instead of working *with* God, humanity now worked *against* God. When humans rebelled against God, work became *toil* (Genesis 3:17).

We feel this toil deeply. Work often feels like we're swimming against the current, pushing through obstacle after obstacle just to move forward a little bit. We feel bored, stressed, overwhelmed, and undervalued, and we go long stretches of time without seeing any payoff from our labors. It would be beautiful if bugs didn't destroy crops, if computers (and people) didn't get viruses, if customers appreciated the employees serving them, and if children obeyed and learned the first time they were instructed. We think we long for a work-free world, but what we really long for is a *toil-free* world.

Fortunately, we serve a God in the business of restoring what man's rebellion broke, and God-honoring work redeems what sin tries to destroy. Often we want our work to highlight our own skills, talents, and sacrifices. We want a job to bring us fulfillment, wealth, and a legacy that honors our efforts. We focus primarily on what we'll get out of our work when God instead offers us something even greater: an invitation. As children of God, we're invited to come alongside our Creator and push back the darkness with our hands, hearts, and minds through our work. Good work brings glory to God as we do what He created us to do.

We're invited to come alongside our Creator and push back the darkness with our hands, hearts, and minds through our work.

God ordained work as a way to worship Him, give purpose to our time, and provide for ourselves. This gives meaning and dignity to even the smallest, most overlooked job. This makes work inherently spiritual, even if we're working outside of official ministry-related occupations. This also means the work we do outside of an official "job" (such as parenting, volunteering, hobbies, etc.) also contains meaning and value.

This view of work frees us from the trap of believing that a job is *only* meaningful if we *feel* it's meaningful. Whether you're running a successful company or wiping a child's nose for the fiftieth time in an hour, God takes great pleasure in seeing His children joyfully and willingly exercising their dominion over earth. There's purpose, value, and dignity *in work itself* because it brings blessing to others and honor to our heavenly Father.[2]

Eternal Excellence

Through our work, we have the opportunity to glorify the Creator of the universe. This is why we should aim to be the best employees, bosses, and workers. We should show up on time, treat others with kindness, be honest, and become as excellent as possible in our fields with the time, talent, and resources God gave us. "Whatever you do, work heartily, as for the Lord and not for men, knowing that from the Lord you will receive the inheritance as your reward. You are serving the Lord Christ" (Colossians 3:23–24).

Being excellent at our jobs isn't about "making it to the top." It's about having an eternal impact. God isn't going to look at our résumés before letting us into heaven, but the Bible does suggest that *how* we use what He gives us here on earth influences our rewards in heaven.

In Matthew 25, Jesus tells us the parable of the talents. A master, who was departing on a journey, left each of his three servants in charge of a certain amount of talents. (A *talent* was a measure of currency back then, but if you appreciate obscure linguistic trivia, the modern English word *talent* is derived from this parable.)

> To one he gave five talents, to another two, to another one, to each according to his ability. Then he went away. (Matthew 25:15)

The servant with the five talents immediately began using them for business and eventually doubled the amount for his master. The servant with the two talents did the same. The servant who'd been given only the one talent, however, dug a hole and buried it. When the master returned, he rewarded the two servants who had wisely used the resources he'd put in their care.

> His master said to him, "Well done, good and faithful servant. You have been faithful over a little; I will set you over much. Enter into the joy of your master." (Matthew 25:21)

The master didn't ask each servant if they had multiplied their talents by doing work they were passionate about. He didn't ask if they had reached for the stars or chased their dreams. He simply rewarded the first two servants for their faithfulness with what he'd given them to steward. They were rewarded because, out of love and devotion to their master, they *did something* with the talents entrusted to them.

The master, though, had a very different reaction to the servant who had buried his talent.

> You wicked and slothful servant! You knew that I reap where I have not sown and gather where I scattered no seed? Then you ought to have invested my money with the bankers, and at my coming I should have received what was my own with interest. (Matthew 25:26–27)

Investing something requires minimal effort—at most, a trip to the bank (or today, a quick log-on to our banking app). It's the most passive way to multiply something. Had the servant done even that, it would've shown that, on some level, the servant respected and cared about his master. It would've been enough. Instead, the third servant only labored enough to dig a hole and put what his master had given him out of sight.

God has entrusted us with an incredibly valuable gift: *life*. With this life, He's given each of us a set of "talents." He's given us time, abilities, personalities, spiritual gifts, resources, and more. In working excellently, you're showing respect and honor for your Creator by *doing something*. Through work, we take what God has given us and multiply it.

Developing Fulfillment

There seem to be two types of people in this world: those who know exactly what they want to be when they grow up and those who will, on their deathbeds, still be trying to figure out what they want to be when they grow up.

My older sister, Lori, falls in the first category. She knew she wanted to be a nurse practically from the day she was born, she began nursing school at seventeen, and she continues working as a nurse to this day. I, on the other hand, fall into the latter category. I've held a wide variety of jobs throughout the years. I've done everything from folding shirts at the Gap to screening calls at a radio station, trying to "discern" my ultimate vocational calling. I still flip-flop sometimes about what I want to do for the rest of my life.

If we find ourselves indecisive or jumping around trying to discover the perfect job, sometimes the best thing we can do is ask God to help us develop fulfillment in the work we're already doing.

One of the jobs I held before comedy and writing transitioned from hobbies to jobbies[3] was teaching music classes. I had studied piano and musical theater for most of my childhood, so I taught private lessons and musical theater classes off and on over the years to support myself and my creative endeavors. When I first began teaching, I didn't like it at all. I counted down the minutes until the end of each class and looked forward to the day when I didn't have to teach ever again. Over time, though, I found myself enjoying the teaching process more and more. As I learned how to teach, I experienced great joy in watching kids and adults discover a new world through music. I loved getting to know my students and their families, and I liked getting to help shape, in some small way, a child's life. I no longer dreaded going to work and often looked forward to lessons and classes. I even considered going back to school for a degree in music education. (And maybe someday I will!)

Satisfaction in my work grew as I saw fruits from my efforts. I felt a deep sense of fulfillment watching my students learn, achieve, and enjoy music, but it took several years of *toil* to get to a place of enjoyment. If you're dissatisfied with your job, it might be helpful to step back and look for ways you've grown in your work, either professionally or personally. Continuous toil without any evidence of progress leads to discouragement and burnout. Sometimes our ability to see the good in our current situation simply requires an attitude adjustment and persistence. Other times, though, it means accepting that a job switch might be necessary. We're going to look briefly at both of these scenarios as we wrap up this chapter.

Means to a Fulfilling End

In chapter 2 we looked at the consequences of "choice overload," and this struggle definitely affects many people who are trying to decide on an occupation.

A couple of hundred years ago, you typically had only a handful of options for jobs. You could farm the back forty, work in a factory, train as an apprentice and enter a trade, or hop on a wagon train heading west and try not to get cholera. Now we have hundreds, if not thousands, of job choices. The sky is no longer the limit. (I think the moon might currently be the limit? Maybe Mars?)

It's difficult to stay put in one job if we think there might be something out there that's *even better*. Amid the sea of memes about dreams, goals, and claiming your destiny, we've come to believe that there might be *one ultimate job* out there that will give us everything we've ever wanted.

That job exists only in the land of unicorns and Pegasus. No career is perfect. Even your dream job will have days, even seasons, of *toil*. From the outside, a different job may look more exciting and rewarding, but once on the inside, you'll probably find the day-to-day struggles aren't terribly different from the one you left. If you don't feel like you're making an impact at your job, sometimes the best thing you can do is stick it out for a while and see if anything changes.

Sometimes a job never provides the fulfillment you want from it but instead gives you the opportunity to do meaningful work and ministry in other areas of life.

My dad started his career as a pilot in the Air Force and later became a pilot for a commercial airline. The words *passion* and *calling* were never once used in connection with his job. In fact, if you were to ask him if he was "called" to be a pilot, he'd probably tell you, "I was called to take care of my family, and being a pilot allowed me to do that."

Though his work didn't leave him overwhelmingly fulfilled, my dad took his job seriously and it showed. In thirty-five years of flying he never once crashed a plane, and he even regaled us occasionally with stories of how he had handled emergency situations calmly and expertly.

Though piloting suited his detail-oriented personality and engineering talents, I later learned my dad always wished he'd become an actor or a surgeon (possibly the two most unrelated fields, but I'm not here to judge). He wasn't given many choices when he finished high school, and by the time he realized there were other options, he had decided it wouldn't be worth the sacrifices necessary to switch careers.

So he accepted his job for what it was: a way to provide for his family and an opportunity to glorify God. He used flying time to engage his copilots in deep discussions about life and faith. On long stretches of days off he homeschooled his children and played an active role in our lives. He lived out his acting dream doing some plays at a community theater, and even his surgeon dreams by removing a fishhook I accidentally cast into my brother's arm.

He made the best of a job that he didn't enjoy, and as his daughter, I reaped many benefits from his persistence and dedication.

Changing Courses

With all that said, it's not wrong to change jobs, and there's definitely a time and a place for a career move. One of the blessings of living in a culture with options is that we *can* recalibrate and change course. If you're stuck in a job you hate, need something that pays better, or discover that you're ill-suited for your current line of work and switching is an option, *do it.* Shifting careers usually takes time and energy and sometimes money, but the end result might be worth the effort. A potential red flag, though, is if changing jobs becomes your immediate default action when things get hard. You may want to dig deeper into the root of your dissatisfaction. (See previous chapter.)

If you're considering a change, make sure your expectations are realistic and you've evaluated the potential sacrifices. If you weigh the risks and trade-offs and decide it's better to stay where you are, that's okay too. There are certainly benefits to staying put and investing in your current position and relationships. We want a "right" answer on something that really comes down to wisdom and preference. Seek the Lord, make your choice, and trust Him with the outcome.

Work is a vital and meaningful part of life, but it's not *all* of life. Do your best to find a job you enjoy, but keep the bigger picture in mind: work is for the glory of God. Remember that your job, whether you love it or tolerate it, doesn't define you completely.

Considerations

1. Where are you with your current job situation? Satisfied? Dissatisfied? Somewhere in between?

2. In what ways might God be using the work you're currently doing to further His kingdom?

3. Why do you think it's tempting to define ourselves by our work? How can you change your thinking?

A Little Bit Extra

Generally, three things need to fall into place in order to confirm a vocational calling: ability, motivation, and opportunity. If one of those things is lacking, then there's a decent chance God is calling you elsewhere.

CHAPTER 5

The Formula for Perfect

"Legalism breeds a sense of entitlement that turns us into complainers."
Tullian Tchividjian, *Jesus + Nothing = Everything*

As you might've gathered by now, I grew up with a decent amount of exposure to Bible Belt culture. My homeschool upbringing added on its own unique brand of Christian subculture, and I had the distinct privilege of coming of age during the *I Kissed Dating Goodbye* (IKDG) movement.

Anyone raised in the church during the late '90s and early 2000s is likely familiar with IKDG and the subsequent "purity movement." If you're not familiar with the book of this name, it was written by a young author and spelled out the "right" way to date/court, or dourt, in the twentieth century for a godly, baggage-free marriage.

Because I was an overachiever, I owned not one but *two* copies of IKDG, and to guarantee no man would ever be tempted to look at me improperly (and thus ruin *both* our chances for a perfect married life later), I took up playing the accordion. (The accordion, I've learned, is pretty much a modern-day chastity belt. They should issue them in high schools as a way to curb teen pregnancy.)

I'm not here to bash the author of IKDG, his intentions, or the fallout, but I do think it's helpful to take a look at what this movement revealed in human nature as a whole: the longing for a guaranteed, perfect outcome.

In this particular case, many of us (bear in mind I'm speaking from the female side here) raised in the church were taught that if we wore the right clothes, behaved a certain way, and followed important rules when dating/courting, God would eventually send us a man who'd never sinned. We'd have satisfying marriages, servant-hearted husbands who treated us like princesses, and lots of perfectly behaved children to homeschool, all because we exercised pristine self-control in our pre-married romantic lives.

Many parents latched on to the rules outlined in the IKDG movement because they themselves had entered into marriage with a lot of hurt and they wanted their children spared that kind of pain. Instead of finding a way to avoid difficulty, however, we just manufactured a different line of spiritual baggage: the baggage of legalism.

Legalism happens when people create rules or commands that aren't given by God, often assuming outcomes that God never promises in the Bible. God never promises us a perfect spouse, or a spouse at all, even if we obey all His commands. Rather than seeking purity and self-control solely out of a desire to honor God through obedience, we sought purity because it promised what we wanted: a completely satisfying marriage and family life.

Many of us love rules and formulas (and essential oils) because they give us confidence that things will go a certain way. We follow diets and health programs that ensure a long, disease-free life. We look for a parenting style that promises perfectly behaved, godly children. We search out a career plan that guarantees a lifetime of fulfillment and financial security. But as we learn more about obedience, we find that earthly blessings aren't the ultimate reward; God Himself is the prize.

As we learn more about obedience, we find that earthly blessings aren't the ultimate reward; God Himself is the prize.

Often our desire for formulas comes out of fear. We fear not living our best life: we're afraid of being the only one left single, the only one without kids, the only one without successful kids, the only one without an exciting career, the only one who hasn't been able to get into shape, the only one (fill in the blank). We fear being left behind and missing out.

If someone offered you a list of things you could do to prevent suffering and guarantee your deepest desires would be met, wouldn't you at least listen? I would. (And I have.) Adulting would be much easier if it came with a comprehensive list of instructions and equations to give us a way of controlling things that are often out of our control.

The problem is that, over time, human-created rules and formulas fail to deliver on their promises. The control we're offered through legalism turns out to be an illusion. I know many women who followed their church's courtship rules to the letter and became discouraged when they found marriage and parenting difficult. Some became resentful when those who had "messed up" went on to have peaceful, happy marriages while they, who had done everything "right," struggled in marriage or never found a spouse.

> Again I saw that under the sun the race is not to the
> swift, nor the battle to the strong, nor bread to the
> wise, nor riches to the intelligent, nor favor to those
> with knowledge, but time and chance happen to
> them all. (Ecclesiastes 9:11)

I've met people who, despite caring for their health, got cancer or another disease. I've met couples who parented diligently, only to have a child rebel against faith and family. Stories like these, where people do everything "right" but still endure unfavorable outcomes, scare us because they expose something we don't always like to acknowledge: God is in control, not us. His plan might include the very trials we fear most and are trying to avoid by doing everything "right."

When the desire for a certain lifestyle, comfort, or outcome sits higher in our priorities than God's call to trust Him, it becomes tempting to buy into legalism to achieve it. Unfortunately, legalism does two things. First, if we follow the rules and get what we want, it creates a sense of self-righteousness and entitlement. Second, it suffocates grace and separates us from God working in our lives. When those around us encounter trials, we wonder subconsciously if their circumstances are due to something they did wrong.

The second mind-set is particularly problematic as we try to love and minister to the hurting. We don't always know how to handle pain and heartache, so we often try to help by "fixing" people's problems with a to-do list. Sometimes when we know something worked for us or someone else, we'll try to replicate those results with an algorithm.

For example, as a single woman in my midthirties, I'm accustomed to being asked "Well, are you putting yourself out there?" when someone learns I'm (still) single. The assumption is that I never leave my cat-filled house and that I expect God to bring Mr. Right directly to my doorstep. (None of those assumptions are true about me. I'm rarely at home, I'm allergic to cats, and I fully expect God to bring Mr. Right behind me in line at Chipotle.)

Based on this assumption, people frequently offer me unsolicited suggestions on how to get a spouse. Usually these ideas are based on something that worked for someone else. Once, a lady told me to use a particular dating app because she had a friend whose neighbor's daughter's former roommate met her husband through it. Someone else told me I needed to volunteer more at my church, because that's how she met her spouse. Another woman told me to hang a pair of men's pants at the end of my bed and pray nightly for God to fill the pants with the perfect man. (I had so many questions when she told me this. Did the kind of pants matter? Like, if I hung a pair of scrubs would I get a doctor? If I put an Iron Man suit at the end of my bed, would I get Robert Downey Jr.? *If* I put a pair of skinny jeans at the end of my bed, would I get a worship pastor?!)

These types of well-meaning but ultimately misguided assumptions and suggestions don't just happen to single people either. A friend of mine who hasn't been able to have kids could create a one-woman show about the assumptions, admonitions, and recommendations offered by Christians on how she and her husband could get pregnant.

When someone walks through a difficult season or doesn't "advance" to the next life stage with their peers, we eagerly search for a solution to give (or an explanation so we can avoid the same scenario), when a listening ear and an offer to bring coffee might be a better way to help.

Legalism and the Holy Spirit

God has given us certain black-and-white commands. Do not murder. Do not bear false witness. Do not steal. Those are pretty cut-and-dried and easy to know where the line falls.

Legalism forms in the gray area. Sometimes following a list of "dos and don'ts" is easier than seeking the Holy Spirit's guidance in each situation. At our core, we *want* a ruler so that we know we're measuring up. We also want to experience control over reliance on God.

Within God's commands, He's given us free will to live our lives the way we see fit, but we often prefer a list of rules so we can know *for sure* we're doing things the right way. For example, He tells parents to raise their kids in the instruction of the Lord (Proverbs 22:6; Ephesians 6:4), but He doesn't specify whether public, private, or homeschooling is the best education option. It'd almost be easier if God said, "Homeschooling is the right way to educate a child!" Then we'd *know* what we're doing is right or wrong. Instead, we need to seek the Holy Spirit to discern God's will and then exercise wisdom to do what's best for ourselves and our family.

Similarly, God gives us instructions on how to live before and after marriage (Hebrews 13:4; Ephesians 5:3; 1 Peter 3:7), but He doesn't say whether modern dating, old-school courting, or arranged marriage is the correct route to the altar. (Would you really want to be told that a website called Plenty of Fish is the *only* way to meet a spouse or that you *have* to marry for that matter?)

This blessing of liberty can result in wondering if we're making the "right" choice. Perhaps just as difficult, it also comes with learning to let others make the choices that are best for them, even if they're different from our own. This freedom requires actively seeking and trusting in God every step of the way, and it requires studying God's Word to know where He's given boundaries.

Instead of providing specific rules for every possible situation, God gives commands addressing the sinful tendencies of our hearts, which allows the gospel to be lived out in any time, place, and culture. Legalism involves trusting and hoping in rules, while liberty encourages us to walk with God and seek the Holy Spirit in every circumstance, trusting His guidance each step of the way and resting in His gift of grace.

The Right Way to Love the Law

Our motivation to obey God's laws must always flow out of gratitude for what Christ did for us through His life, death, and resurrection. The more we understand God's holiness, the offensiveness of our sin, and the magnitude of Jesus' sacrifice, the more we'll recognize that even our best actions will never be enough to repay this debt (Isaiah 64:6), much less earn us credits toward cashing in extra blessings here on earth.

When we lose sight of the enormity of our sin and Christ's redeeming sacrifice, our attitude dangerously shifts from one of gratitude to one of entitlement. *Because* I raised my children this way, I *deserve* to have final say in the choices they make as adults. *Because* I didn't date carelessly, I *deserve* a perfect marriage. *Because* I ate well and exercised consistently, I *deserve* a long, healthy life. The moment we begin obeying rules because we expect them to bring a certain earthly outcome, we set ourselves up for disappointment and disillusionment.

To determine our underlying motivation for obedience, we can ask ourselves this question: "Is knowing that this action obeys and honors God enough?" If I'm honest, many times my answer has been "No." Honoring God with obedience looks a whole lot more appealing if I also get an amazing spouse, healthy kids, a good-sized bank account, and a meaningful career out of it. Fortunately, God can handle our honesty.

To avoid falling into legalism, we have to recalibrate how we view God's instructions. We often see them as keeping us *away* from the things we want, but God actually gave us laws as a way of providing freedom. He designed us, and each of His commands was given in our best interest. He didn't give us laws to *prevent* us from enjoying life; He gave them to *allow* us full, abundant living. Freedom always requires boundaries of some sort. For the artist, it's the canvas. For the athlete, it's the playing field. For children, it's the yard. Without any boundaries, chaos and confusion abound.

When I taught music at an elementary school, I had three rules when students stepped into my classroom: "Listen and obey, be kind, and have fun!" (And yes, more than one student pointed out that "listen and obey" are technically *two* rules.) If they weren't listening and obeying, pandemonium reigned. If they weren't kind to each other, much of class was spent dealing with hurt feelings and tears. When they listened, obeyed, and treated each other kindly, it freed us to have fun. The first two rules created an orderly environment that invited them to love music and enjoy learning so we could play musical games, use instruments, and sing songs. (Granted, they didn't always have fun, as quarter notes and scales can get boring even in the most creative of settings.)

Living according to God's law often brings earthly blessings, which is why legalism can be so sneaky. At the risk of sounding like the end of a *VeggieTales* episode, I'll say this: His way for us is the best way. Those who diligently love, discipline, and teach their children about Jesus regularly see their kids grow up to love the Lord as adults and lead fruitful, meaningful lives. Adopting healthy habits frequently leads to more energy and fewer doctor visits. Working hard generally leads to advancement and feeling fulfilled in your job.

While obeying God's law ***sometimes*** *brings earthly prosperity, it* ***always*** *brings spiritual prosperity.*

While obeying God's law *sometimes* brings earthly prosperity, it *always* brings spiritual prosperity. Obedience allows us to see into the heart of God and grow in our love and knowledge of our Creator. And it opens our eyes to see His blessings for what they are: beautiful, undeserved gifts from our Father.

Psalm 119, the longest chapter in the Bible, is basically an extensive love song to God's law. I'm not going to put the entire passage in here because it would put me over my word count for the book, but let's look at a few excerpts, and I highly encourage you to read the whole chapter on your own. (All verses below are from the NIV.)

> I rejoice in following your statutes as one rejoices in great riches. (v. 14)

> Be good to your servant while I live, that I may obey your word. (v. 17)

> Turn my heart toward your statutes and not toward selfish gain. (v. 36)

> The arrogant mock me unmercifully, but I do not turn from your law. (v. 51)

> At midnight I rise to give you thanks for your righteous laws. (v. 62)

> May your unfailing love be my comfort, according to your promise to your servant. (v. 76)

My soul faints with longing for your salvation, but I have put my hope in your word. (v. 81)

To all perfection I see a limit, but your commands are boundless. (v. 96)

Because I love your commands more than gold, more than pure gold, and because I consider all your precepts right, I hate every wrong path. (vv. 127–128)

Your promises have been thoroughly tested, and your servant loves them. (v. 140)

The psalmist loved, even *lived for*, God's law because through it he grew closer to God. God revealed Himself to humans through His Word, and by His Word and commands, we learn who God is and how we can glorify Him. Learning to delight in His commands and obey out of our love for Jesus frees us to embrace the outcomes, even if they're not exactly what we wanted.

Considerations

1. Think about your life. What, if taken away (or never given), would make life not worth living to you?

2. To what extremes have you tried to control or avoid a particular scenario?

3. How can you grow in your love for God's law?

A Little Bit Extra

I am a recovering legalist. I loved rules and judging those who didn't follow them perfectly. Fortunately, there is grace for Pharisees and legalism addicts. If you've been caught up in loving rules and the resulting feelings of self-righteousness, ask God to forgive you and grant you empathy and understanding for people with backgrounds and perspectives different from your own. Then move forward in kindness and compassion.

CHAPTER 6

I Can Do All the Things

"For every winner, there are dozens of losers.
Odds are you're one of them."

E. L. Kersten

I had a relatively adversity-free childhood. I lived in a safe suburban neighborhood, had minimal exposure to cultures and worldviews outside my own, and did activities that catered to my talents and interests. My world was small and sheltered.

Of course, even the most protected kids aren't safeguarded against *all* failure and rejection. I almost always froze up during piano competitions, I consistently got picked last for the kickball team at youth group gatherings, and my parents insisted I finish out the swim team season, even after I pretended to drown to get out of one of the practices. (I was "extra" before "extra" was a thing.)

Still, for the majority of my childhood, failure, rejection, and resiliency weren't part of my everyday life. That changed, though, when I went to college. I barely passed my first college algebra test, and the professor didn't even bother writing an encouraging note like "You'll do better next time!" on my paper. He just marked all the ones I got wrong with a red *X* and wrote the final grade at the top of the page. The monster!

Growing up, I did a lot of musical theater. Most of the shows I performed in were produced by a local community theater. My dream was to one day be a Broadway leading lady, but as I got older and started auditioning for shows at other theaters, I wasn't cast and often didn't even receive a callback. Humiliated and defeated by the constant rejection, I soon realized that if I couldn't beat out the competition for a show at a small black-box theater in North Texas, I probably didn't stand a chance in New York City. A voice teacher from college confirmed this suspicion when she told me straight up that my vocal range wasn't going to cut it for Broadway and, unless I could dance circles around everyone else (I couldn't), I might want to consider taking my career goals in another direction. This was a sucker punch to my eighteen-year-old soul. Was there even life outside of singing while doing jazz squares?! It's silly to think about it now, but back then I honestly didn't know.

The bubbles on my bubble-wrapped life continued popping after college when I moved to Los Angeles and started taking comedy and improv classes. I really wanted to do sketch writing and possibly write for *Saturday Night Live* one day (leave it to me to pick the one career track even less realistic than Broadway), but many schools required you to pass several improv classes before they moved you to the sketch comedy track. I learned pretty quickly that I wasn't super-gifted at improv, and I never made it far enough to even get into the sketch classes. In addition, I was now constantly around people who didn't share my worldview, and I found myself getting frustrated or retreating completely when I encountered disagreement of any kind.

Everyone in Los Angeles had huge dreams, and nobody really cared about any dreams other than their own. Back home, I was a decent-sized fish in a pond of similar fish. Now I was a minnow in the ocean of reality. I came to the unfortunate realization that, while I was special to my family and a few close friends, to the rest of the world I was unimportant and inconsequential.

Looking back, my twenties were basically a series of humiliating events connected by trips to Chipotle. I realized my talents weren't anything special, my dreams weren't going anywhere, not everyone wants to be friends when you don't agree on everything, and the longer I floundered figuring things out, the more credit card debt I amassed. (Perhaps I should've cut back on my trips to Chipotle ... or at least skipped the guac.)

Each failure felt like God had abandoned me. Wasn't I special? Hadn't God set me aside to do great things like I'd been told? Why had God given me a dream but not the talent to achieve it? What lesson was I supposed to be learning from all this failure and rejection anyway? Surely if I knew what I was doing, life wouldn't be this hard.

One of my favorite Bible verses that frequently gets taken out of context in our culture is Philippians 4:13, which reads, "I can do all things through Christ who strengthens me" (NKJV). I love this verse, but our success-oriented culture has extracted it out of a larger context and given it a narrow, one-sided application. We've changed it to mean, "I can *get what I want* through Christ who strengthens me." We look at that verse and think, *Because I have Christ, I can make that touchdown, I can get that promotion, I can score that callback, etc.*

Christ can, and does, give us the strength to succeed and accomplish great things. We strive for excellence because we serve an excellent God. This quest for excellence comes with wonderful success sometimes, and it's good to recognize that God ultimately gives us the talent, drive, and means to achieve great things.

More overlooked (at the very least, less preached in my own experience) is the reality that God gives us strength to face failure and hardship. Because you have Christ, you have the strength to handle blowing the final play of the game, losing out on your dream job, or never getting cast in anything—and not only to survive, but to thrive and joyfully embrace life.

Before Paul's bold declaration that he could do all things through Christ's strength, he said this: "I know how to be brought low, and I know how to abound. In any and every circumstance, I have learned the secret of facing plenty and hunger, abundance and need" (v. 12).

Sometimes God gives us the strength to nail an interview and land the job of our dreams. Other times, though, He gives us the strength to make it through another day at a job we can't stand. Both are God's grace. Getting through life, I've learned, takes something I call godly grit.* And unfortunately, this godly grit is developed through hard circumstances, not easy ones.

Learning Grit

After almost ten years of teaching piano lessons, I noticed a difference between students who stuck with it and students who quit. About two years into studying music, kids who didn't show a lot of natural talent in the beginning, but who had practiced

---

*   I thought I coined this term, but I ran it through Google to double-check that assumption. Not only did I *not* coin this phrase, but based on the number of search results, I'm the last one to have thought of it.

regularly, suddenly began advancing quickly. After two years of struggle, something clicked, and almost overnight piano became significantly easier. Even more interesting, the struggling gave them a stronger sense of pride in their musical abilities. They enjoyed not only playing piano but the learning process as well. Because they had a track record of overcoming challenges, they didn't feel instantly defeated when they encountered difficult new concepts. In short, they had learned grit.

On the flip side, I noticed the students who advanced quickly in the beginning often hit a wall after a year or two. Even the most naturally talented musician eventually reaches a level where the music requires diligent practice and effort. These inherently gifted students almost always wanted to quit when the songs became challenging. Because they hadn't learned how to handle challenges in their early lessons, the effort felt agonizing and, as one student put it, "like a mortal punishment." They only enjoyed music when it was easy, not because they'd seen the payoff of their hard work. They hadn't learned grit.

> For the righteous falls seven times and rises again,
> but the wicked stumble in times of calamity.
> (Proverbs 24:16)

Adulting requires learning how to fall and get back up again, and again, and again. Godly grit comes from understanding that struggles, setbacks, and disappointments are not only parts of life but that God uses them to shape us, deepen our faith, and prepare us for our callings (Ephesians 2:10; 1 Peter 5:10). If your childhood bore any resemblance to mine, then you're probably just now learning to face life-altering disappointments and setbacks in your twenties and thirties. Let's look at ten ways to shift our perspective on struggle and develop godly grit.

Expect Hardship

I know this sounds incredibly pessimistic, but Jesus Himself tells us that this world will contain troubles (John 16:33). Western comforts have lulled us into the false assumption that life is meant to be easy and the hard moments few. In reality, much of life is hard, and the easy moments are the exceptions.

Hopefully this revelation won't send you into a tailspin of angst but instead prepare you so difficult circumstances don't catch you off guard. Though unwise actions and decisions may have negative consequences, many hardships and failures are simply parts of life and don't necessarily mean you're doing anything wrong. Trials are par for the course.[1]

As believers, we're even called to find joy in our hardships (James 1:2–3) because we know they're being used to test our faith, produce maturity, and mold us into Christ's image. Some aspects of Christlike character, such as perseverance and long-suffering, can be achieved *only* through enduring tough times.

Depend on God

The general complaint that younger generations are too dependent on their parents probably has some truth to it. However, we *should* be dependent on our heavenly Father no matter how old we get. Right after telling His followers they'll experience trouble in this world, Jesus reassures them (and us) that He has overcome the world (John 16:33).

When you experience difficulty, start by going directly to the One who has overcome the world. Before searching online, calling home, or crowdsourcing the issue to Facebook, bring your trial before the throne of your heavenly Father.

Whether it's a job you lost, a test you bombed, or a relationship that ended abruptly, failure hurts—often deeply. Christians don't have to fake a sense of happiness about life. If you don't believe me, read through the book of Psalms. We can be honest about our hurt and struggles while still trusting God. Grit doesn't mean you ignore the feelings of sadness and disappointment; it simply means you recognize that God's ultimate purpose will be done through your setbacks.

Ask "What's Next?"

Rather than giving over to self-pity, ask yourself, "What's next?" I stole this one from my friend Johnnie, who sustained life-threatening injuries to his legs from an improvised explosive device during his second deployment to Afghanistan.[2]

Rather than ask "Why me?" he decided to ask a different question about life: "What's next?"

Obstacles, especially a long string of them, can make us short-sighted. When you're hating your job, struggling with loneliness, or going through the motions day to day without any hope of change, it's hard to envision life getting better.

By asking "What's next?" we recognize this failure or hardship isn't the end of our story; it's simply one part of it. This attitude opens our eyes to the bigger picture. Over time, we see how God can redeem even the most horrific circumstances.

This failure or hardship isn't the end of our story; it's simply one part of it. This attitude opens our eyes to the bigger picture.

Though your current heartbreak may feel permanent, you can and will move forward. Hardships will undoubtably change you, but keeping a long-term perspective will prevent them from destroying you.

Look at Adversity through Eternal Lenses

We like to say "Life is too short!" But sometimes, especially in the middle of painful seasons, life can feel very, very long.

Adversity isn't fun, but as a child of God your trials, both big and small, have an expiration date. In addition to asking, "What's next?" ask yourself, "Will this matter in one year? Ten years? Forty? A hundred?" Some of your trials may resolve during your time on earth. Other struggles, however, may stick with you until you enter heaven's gates. In light of eternity, though, fifty, sixty, or even seventy years isn't very long.

Our life isn't over until we take our final breath, and if we're in Christ, that last exhale simply ushers us into our heavenly beginning. We want things to get better quickly, but some of our greatest victories will happen through long-term battles.

Appreciate the Bottom

When I first started out in comedy, I asked a seasoned comic the best way to get ahead in the business. His answer was simple, "Get onstage as much as possible, no matter the audience." He told me new comics often want to jump right to bigger shows with large crowds, but the *real* lessons in comedy were learned by doing shows in difficult, non-advantageous settings. Good crowds don't sharpen your skills, he said—hard crowds do that. Then, once you're a good comedian, the advancement takes care of itself.

Many of us don't want to do "low rung" work, but there's something to be said for starting at the very bottom and working our way up.

If we begin at the top, we'll miss the lessons available to us on all the other rungs. Ascending at a reasonable pace helps us acclimate to the altitude of success, where the air is thinner and the stakes often higher. (Success generally means having more people watch you fail.)

If you're in a low-level position at work or elsewhere, devote yourself to learning as much as you can. Whether it's figuring out how to deal with customers, fine-tuning your time-management skills, or just understanding how to responsibly spend a smaller paycheck, a lot can be learned on the bottom step of the ladder.

Develop Thick Skin and a Tender Heart

Sometimes our heartache comes from dealing with difficult people. Humans, as you're probably already aware, aren't always kind, and it's impossible to avoid conflict completely. Whether it's passive-aggressive family members, blunt coworkers, rude drivers, or a total stranger in Panera who yells at you for pointing out the open cashier (who tried multiple times to get the person's attention), people can quickly drain us. When it comes to dealing with humans, it helps to develop thick skin and a tender heart.[3]

In Romans, Paul instructed Christ followers to live at peace with others as much as possible (12:18). Over the years, I've learned to ask myself three questions when I'm the recipient of hostility: (a) Is God using this to point out something I truly need to change?; (b) Does their anger and offense reflect something they're dealing with and I just happen to be in their crosshairs?; *and* (c) How do I best show kindness and restore peace with the soul treating me this way?

Try to be slow in getting offended and quick in extending grace. If someone causes you to have a knee-jerk reaction, that person controls you. That person has all the power. Instead, pull an "Elsa" and let it go. Though this strategy may feel like it's giving bad behavior a pass, by choosing a calm response and keeping a level head, you remain free to live your life.

Be Teachable

Though we don't need to let the opinions and critiques of everyone we encounter control our lives, we *do* need people who can lovingly speak truth into our lives.

Teachability means opening ourselves up to correction, but even constructive criticism can hurt because it brings us face to face with our flaws, and that's never fun. I'd much prefer a world where only my positive qualities were noticed and highlighted, but alas, that isn't the world in which I live. Nor is constant praise really what's best for me.

During the first few episodes in each season of *American Idol*, we see terrible singers with over-inflated egos meet reality. Sometimes the negative feedback from the judges catches the aspiring singers completely by surprise. Either no one had been bold enough to tell them the truth or they were too proud to listen when someone *did* tell them they couldn't carry a tune. When they finally went for their dreams, they became a national laughingstock.

Our natural instinct is to make excuses or get defensive when someone corrects us, but adopting an attitude of teachability puts us on the track to growth and maturity. We need to take ownership of our actions and be humble enough to receive input about where we can improve.

Do Something

Sometimes life comes to a stagnating halt. We hit the ceiling at work, friends get busy with their own lives, and long periods of time go by where nothing new happens.

A few years ago, US Navy Admiral William McRaven gave a speech that went viral; it was titled "If You Want to Change the World, Start Off by Making Your Bed."[4] By making your bed, you begin the day by *doing* something, which gives you a sense of accomplishment and motivates you to do *more* things the rest of the day. Plus, if your day is terrible, at least you come home to a bed that's made.

If you're stuck in a rut, pick something small and make yourself do it. Walk to the end of your street and back. Clean one shelf in your closet. Learn to say something simple in another language. Turning off Netflix and leaving the couch might be the hardest parts of moving forward in life, but big changes happen through tiny actions, and tiny actions require *doing* something.

Laugh

Despite dabbling in the comedic arts for most of my adulthood, I spent many years taking life way too seriously. If I bombed a show, I'd beat myself up for days. If I tried to organize a game night and only one person showed up, I'd spend weeks feeling rejected. If a video I posted didn't get many views, I'd dwell on what an embarrassing failure I was as an artist. I put too much weight on small things. Though my job involved getting people to laugh at me, I still needed to learn to laugh at myself.

One time, after a particularly rough show at a church,** I called a friend to mope about my lack of talent.

"Was it really that bad?" my friend asked, knowing I'm prone to hyperbolic exaggeration.

"I thought they were going to stone me with the clicky pens from the backs of the chairs!"

** Until starting stand-up, I didn't know I possessed the ability to get five hundred people to collectively despise me within thirty seconds of walking onstage. But sometimes I get standing ovations, so it all balances out.

Something about the visual of getting driven offstage by people hurling church clicky pens at me made me laugh. And it made my friend laugh. We laughed hard, and for the first time, I was able to let my failure roll off my back.

Once I learned to laugh at myself and find humor in situations that didn't tip in my favor, I became less stressed about every little thing.

Once I learned to laugh at myself and find humor in situations that didn't tip in my favor, I became less stressed and anxious about every little thing. I didn't dread life or failure as much. Not every circumstance calls for joking and levity, of course, but finding the humor in everyday life, especially in our mistakes and failures, makes the ride so much more enjoyable. Laughter reminds us that our hope isn't ultimately in everything going our way, and humor keeps the weight of our circumstances from crushing us.

Count Your Blessings

Yes, it's cliché, but during tough times it helps to take a step back and praise God for everything He's given us. Instead of focusing constantly on everything that's going wrong, take time each day to remember what's going right. We might find our "gratitude attitude" changes our entire outlook on life.

Considerations

1. What kinds of failure, hardships, and setbacks have you experienced in life? How did you handle those times, and what valuable lessons did they teach you?

2. Why do you think criticism is so hard for people to receive?

3. How are you doing with developing godly grit?

A Little Bit Extra

In light of eternity, even the most gut-wrenching disappointment will be all but forgotten when we finally see the face of Jesus. I'm not sure if we'll fail in heaven or if we'll simply have perfect resiliency. Either way, it will be perfect.

CHAPTER 7

Finding Rest in an Anti-Sabbath World

"Rest provides fine-tuning for hearing God's message amidst the static of life."

Shelly Miller, *Rhythms of Rest*

Recently I decided to take an afternoon reprieve from looking at my phone, just like the mental health experts recommend. I'd become increasingly and compulsively glued to it, and after feeling convicted about the amount of time I spend on it (shout-out to my iPhone's no-nonsense weekly screen report), I decided it was time to take a brief technology hiatus. To avoid temptation, I put my phone in the basement, closed the door, and focused on other things for a few hours. I'll admit, I was a little bit proud of myself for resisting multiple urges to go in and sneak a peek to see if I'd missed anything.

When I finally returned to grab it, I had a text from a comedian friend who had to drop out of an upcoming show and needed someone to replace him. It had been a slow work month for me, and the honorarium of this show would've covered a good portion of my bills. Unfortunately, because I hadn't responded in a timely fashion (within a couple of hours), the show went to someone else. My little technology Sabbath cost me meaningful, life-sustaining work.

Kristin, this is a really depressing way to start a chapter.

I know, but I promise I'll circle back to this and leave you with a happy ending.

Always On

We live in a fast-paced world that never really stops. Millennials are called the "burnout generation," with many struggling to find the motivation to both go to work and complete basic adulting tasks like grocery shopping or getting to the post office.[1] Because we're so accessible through our devices, both our work *and* our social lives stay with us 24/7, requiring us to be a little bit "on" all the time. On a number of occasions, I've found myself glancing at my phone *one last time* before going to bed, only to get caught up in answering emails or falling down a clickbait rabbit hole. (I don't care how many times I have to click "next" to get to the point of the article; I *have* to know what brought the ER doctor to tears when he went into the patient's room!)

Most of us *want* to detach and rest, but we're also aware that unplugging completely can mean getting behind or missing out. Despite our perceived lack of work ethic as a generation, many of us actually believe that in order to live a life of impact we must always be doing something. Whether it's taking steps to further our careers or better ourselves as humans, we are constantly striving to become *better*. And this nonstop striving creates exhaustion.

God didn't design us to continuously live at this pace. In the Old Testament, the Israelites were commanded to set aside the last day of the week and consecrate it as a holy day of rest called the Sabbath (Exodus 34:21). God modeled this for us in Genesis when He spent six days creating and then rested from His work on the seventh (Genesis 2:2). The Sabbath was meant to give those bearing God's image a break from the regular efforts of work and self-sufficiency. It was meant to be "Father's Day,"[2] a chance to refocus on what truly mattered: their relationship with Yahweh.

While Jesus is our ultimate Sabbath rest (Hebrews 4:8–10; Matthew 12:1–8) and we're no longer commanded to officially observe a weekly Sabbath day (Colossians 2:16), the pattern for meaningful rest is demonstrated for us throughout the Bible. In Psalm 23, we see God leading us to green pastures and quiet waters to restore our souls. In Matthew, Jesus offers rest to all who labor and are heavy laden (Matthew 11:28). Jesus even frequently retreated from crowds and His ministry to restore His spirit and spend meaningful time with His Father (Matthew 14:23; Mark 6:31–32). The theme of rest, specifically finding rest under the wing of our Creator, threads itself through God's Word.

It *is* possible to find rest in a culture that pushes us to do more, be more, and accomplish more, but to understand how to rest effectively, we need to ask ourselves three things: What are we resting from?; Who are we resting in?; and How do we rest?

What Are We Resting From?

First, by taking a Sabbath, we're resting *from* labor and toil—not just physical labor, but mental as well. In the book of 1 Peter, we're told to cast our worries onto Jesus, because He cares for us (5:7). God knows that sometimes our burdens are less physical in nature and more emotional or spiritual. Are you dealing with anxiety about the future? Hopelessness? Debt? Political uncertainty? Criticism about your inability to adult?

While it may be difficult to completely turn our brains off when something weighs heavily, committing to rest from these thoughts is a tangible way of casting our cares upon the Lord. While we rest, He carries our burdens.

Second, we need to rest *from* the hamster wheel of approval and affirmation we seek in places other than God. Some of us look for approval from our work, some of us find it on Instagram, and some of us get it through our hobbies or social groups. We need time away from these places to remember that we already have the only approval we need through the sacrifice of Christ.

Who Are We Resting In?

If we're moving *away* from something, we're automatically going *toward* something else. A Sabbath may be absent of *work*, but it's not absent of *purpose*. We must know what we're moving *toward* in our Sabbath; otherwise, we'll spend our designated rest time "puttering about," as my grandmother would say. (Although sometimes "puttering about" can be relaxing and restful.) This is a Christian book and I'm not trying to trick you, so the answer is, of course, we're meant to use our Sabbath to move toward Jesus.

By taking a Sabbath, we're acknowledging the all-sufficiency of Jesus. He's our peace, our burden carrier, our ultimate approval. Our

Sabbath rest celebrates that our works don't save us, the opinions of others don't define us, and our trials don't have the final say.

Our Sabbath rest celebrates that our works don't save us, the opinions of others don't define us, and our trials don't have the final say.

We receive a huge amount of pressure from society to live up to our full potential. A Sabbath reorients us toward Jesus; without Him our potential means nothing at all.

How Do We Rest?

Right now, #selfcare posts flood my social media feed. I have one acquaintance who posts so frequently about her self-care that I wonder if she's doing any #jobcare.

A true Sabbath allows us to be filled up so we can effectively pour out the other six days of the week. And what we fill ourselves up with will determine what we pour out.

When trying to figure out how to structure a Sabbath, it may help to ask, "What will help prepare my body, mind, and soul for what God's calling me to do this week?"

I've heard several people suggest that our Sabbath "activity" should be something different from what we do most of the week. If you sit at a desk every day, go do something a little bit physical. If you're constantly around people during the week, perhaps it's better to retreat somewhere quiet and reflect, read, and journal. If you work from home and your week consists largely of solitude, it may be rejuvenating to go grab coffee with a friend or engage in a hobby away from your house.

And though a Sabbath isn't meant to be a day devoted to pampering ourselves, if you've been chasing kids or lugging suitcases around during a work trip all week, a bubble bath or massage *might* be the best thing to help you refocus and remember God's goodness.

For some of us, finding the rhythm of incorporating rest into our weekly schedules will come easily. For others, it will take some planning and practice to avoid getting drawn back into the rat race of life.

Because I'm easily distracted, I have to loosely plan out my Sabbath ahead of time or else one of two things happens: I spend the whole day wandering around Netflix and playing Bubble Pop on my phone, or I get bored and start working. Neither of those scenarios leaves me feeling filled up and ready to pour out. Also, because my regular workday is unpredictable and lacks structure, creating a plan for my Sabbath allows my mind to rest. If I can't make a whole day of rest happen, I try to carve out a few "mini-Sabbaths" throughout the week. I'll schedule in time to get together with some friends for a movie, block out an hour to take a walk and listen to a podcast, or go to a jiu-jitsu class.*

Your designated time of rest will likely change over time. Seasons of life (work, home, or responsibilities) and interests will impact how you structure your Sabbath. For example, unless parents of toddlers have someone to watch their kids, they can't take a day off from caring for their young children, because the little ones will immediately find all the sharp objects and run around with them pointy side up. The goal isn't to hold tightly to a specific rest routine but to put into action a time of rest that helps you hold tightly to the beauty of your Savior the rest of the week.

The Greater Good

My dad once told me a fable about two lumberjacks who competed to see who could cut down the most trees. The first lumberjack, an older man, was known to be the most skilled and productive woodcutter in the area. The second lumberjack was younger but eager to prove that he could out-chop his older counterpart. They decided to cut down as many trees as possible in twelve hours, and whoever had the highest tree count at the end would be declared the winner. (Greenpeace would *not* approve of this tale.)

The contest started and they both began chopping down trees. The younger man went nonstop, incredibly anxious to win. From across the forest, he noticed the old man would chop for only

---

* I started jiu-jitsu after nearly getting mugged at knifepoint while in Costa Rica. The full story will have to wait for another book, but the experience gave me more street cred than I ever could've hoped for.

forty-five minutes; then for the final fifteen minutes of each hour, he would sit down.

If he keeps stopping, I'll definitely win, thought the junior lumberjack.

At the end of the twelve hours, the younger woodcutter was shocked to discover that, despite his frequent rests, the older man won by quite a bit.

"How is that possible?" the younger man asked the older. "You took so many breaks!"

"My boy, I wasn't taking a break for those fifteen minutes," explained the older man. "I was sharpening my ax."

Taking some designated time each week to rest requires us to pause our work, which seems counterproductive in a world keen on pushing people to reach their full potential. I've often heard people praised for their strong and unwavering work ethic, but I've yet to hear anyone praised for their ability to take a day off.

It seems logical that stepping back from our work for a little while might put us behind, cause us to be forgotten, or make us miss out. That might happen in the short term, but refocusing our hearts, minds, and bodies away from the daily grind and back toward God sharpens our axes so we can be more effective in every sphere of life. Taking time to remember God's place in our lives keeps us from burning out, growing cynical in our daily labors, or becoming all-consumed by them.

When I put away my phone for a few hours to rest from my growing technology addiction, it initially felt like a loss because I missed out on a job opportunity. Really, though, my rest was a success. First, another comedian got work that he or she might've needed just as much as (or more than) I did. Second, I truly felt rested and rejuvenated after focusing on something other than my phone for an extended period of time. Since I didn't have my phone to constantly occupy my mind, I thought of new comedy ideas, friends I needed to catch up with, and deep spiritual questions I wanted answered. And though I lost out on a job, God provided me the means to pay all my bills for that month through another opportunity. Even when we're not working, God still is. (I told you the chapter would have a happy ending! And an ending doesn't get any happier than the God of the universe doing work on our behalf while we take a rest.)

Rest is an exercise in trusting God and believing that He is better than anything the world can give us. And in this day and age, it often starts by simply turning off our phones.

Considerations

1. Do you set aside time to rest each week? Why, or why not?

2. Why do you think God prescribes rest for His children?

3. How might a Sabbath rest look for you?

A Little Bit Extra

Our primary purpose on earth is to glorify and enjoy God. Resting from all the bright and momentary distractions of the world allows us to remember that most important part of our existence.

CHAPTER 8

The Social Media Monster

"One of the great uses of Twitter and Facebook will be to prove at the Last Day that prayerlessness was not from lack of time."

John Piper

It was the fall of 2004 and I was less than two semesters away from graduating from Southern Methodist University with my degree in journalism. I can't remember the details of what we were discussing, but the topic of a new "online social network" called Facebook came up in one of my journalism classes. Apparently, some kid at Harvard created the site to promote connecting individuals via the internet, and he'd made this network available to certain universities, mine being one of them.

We must not have had a pressing assignment, because the professor let us log on to the classroom computers and explore the new site. As we clicked around the program and (a few of us) created our first social media profiles, I decided this whole system of keeping track of people through the internet felt chaotic and impersonal.

"This is weird," I muttered to the students sitting around me. "I don't think this will ever catch on."

It's the funniest thing I've ever said.

Now, less than two decades after declaring Facebook would never amount to anything, checking Facebook is as natural to me as breathing. In fact, my life is so littered with online distractions that in order to work on this book each day, I had to log out of all social media accounts on my computer, make sure my password was "forgotten" so I couldn't get back on with a single click, and put my phone in a different room or turn it to airplane mode. Then, I set a timer and forced myself to focus on doing work, and only work, until that timer went off. (Parenting myself in my thirties is hard but worth it.)

If I don't put up strict boundaries, my morning routine often starts with a "procrastination loop" on my phone. I wake up, look at and respond to text messages, and then I check Facebook, Instagram, my personal email, my work email, WhatsApp, and occasionally I'll throw in a visit to YouTube, Twitter, or my junk email to check for coupons that might be relevant to my life. (I've miraculously managed to avoid the lures of Snapchat and Pinterest. I had TikTok for a couple of weeks until I learned about all the security risks involved with the app, so unfortunately, I'll have to achieve viral dance fame some other way.)

When I lazily scroll through my various feeds, I "ooh" over the new baby of a woman I've never met, roll my eyes at someone's petty rant about the bad service at a local restaurant (they didn't even have the decency to use #firstworldproblems in their outburst!), and grow saddened by a tragedy that occurred a few states away. I take in posts about human trafficking, pictures of war-torn countries halfway around the world, and fearful political rants. Mixed in with all the negative posts are perfectly filtered selfies taken in exotic locations, engagement announcements, and beautiful photos of happy families going about their seemingly perfect lives.

When I'm finished checking everything, before I know it, I've spent nearly an hour on my phone and enough time has passed that it's *possible* something new has come up on one of those platforms, so I refresh and check them again, thus creating the loop.

By the time I get out of bed I've experienced excitement, joy, sadness, jealousy, apathy, outrage, and judgment, largely directed toward people I barely know and situations out of my control. I feel distracted, anxious, overwhelmed, useless, scattered, sad, and behind, all before I've even had any fair-trade coffee.

We all know that's a terrible way to start the day, and studies agree that kicking off your morning with a social media binge is like consuming a mental bowl of glass shards.[1] Still, it's part of the morning routine for many of us. Or we surely get to it eventually.

The Kingdom of Social Media

Several years ago, I was scheduled to go to Bolivia to visit an international school needing a music teacher. As I researched etiquette and customs for the area, I learned it's polite to put away phones and cameras in certain regions of the country because many of the indigenous people groups don't want their photos taken. Each picture, they believe, steals a part of your soul.[2] *If a picture steals part of your soul*, I thought, *then all of Western culture has uploaded their souls onto Instagram.*

Though pictures won't whittle away our actual souls, social media gives each of us platforms to create a world devoted to ourselves, and many of us are building thriving online kingdoms.[3] And social media feeds narcissism by putting the user at the center of the story. Studies show that in face-to-face interactions, we usually talk about ourselves only 30 to 40 percent of the time. In our online interactions, though, we talk about ourselves closer to 80 percent of the time.[4]

So we carefully pick and choose what to share in our online space, getting a little rush of dopamine with each "like" or "heart."[5] If something doesn't get the response we want, we can wait a little while and covertly remove it, sparing ourselves the humiliation of visible unpopularity and keeping the integrity of our online self-shrine intact. (I've even caught myself cyberstalking my own profiles to make sure they look impressive to others.)

When social media first entered the world, we used it to escape from "real" life. Now as we've gradually put more and more of our identity into the number of "likes," "follows," and "retweets" our posts receive, "real" life has become a way of escaping social media. Even when we manage to pull ourselves away from our various platforms, though, we often view "real" life as a way to generate post-able content. And let's be honest. Would we *still* want to get up at the crack of dawn to hike twelve miles up a mountain if we had no way of showing the world what we accomplished? (And how flawless we looked doing it?)

My social media kingdom also gives me a sense of control that most of life doesn't offer. I can't control the weather, the global economy, my coworker's attitude, or the latest E. coli outbreak at Chipotle. But doggonit, I can make sure my online friends see me as funny, well-traveled, generous, and effortlessly beautiful. I can build a moat around my kingdom by unfollowing angry people, blocking anyone who disagrees with me, and making sure my feed only shows me funny memes and viewpoints I already agree with.

Unfortunately, as our online feudal system has grown, the foundation of our offline life has crumbled. Social media has been around long enough for us to observe the negative effects it's having on our brains. We know that constantly seeing everyone's best and brightest moments brings us FOMO (fear of missing out) and dissatisfaction with our own life.[6] The overexposure to tragic stories and graphic media either desensitizes us or makes us anxious and afraid. Our short, over-edited online interactions are chipping away at our ability to listen, care, and converse with people face to face.

While technology has the unique ability to connect people, one glance through the comments section of any popular YouTube video shows that rather than fostering an online Shangri-la, the combination of anonymity and free speech has created a digital race of merciless trolls (who seem to grow more vicious by the day). Our social media also exposes us to another not-so-fun world, one made up of isolation and loneliness. We're made for *connectedness*, but not this kind. Rather than supplementing our "real life" relationships, social media "friendships" are beginning to replace them.

Finally, social media creates a sense of chaos and unrest. It's good to be aware, but the constant scream of information, opinions, and arguing brings disorder to our minds. Increasingly becoming a place of mayhem where we input a world's worth of information with a limited ability to act upon it, social media left unchecked gives us the combined sense of helplessness and hopelessness.

Addicted to Interaction

Here's the thing: I'm probably not telling you anything you don't already know. We're constantly seeing new studies and articles about the negative effects of constant social media interaction, ironically while we're using social media, but I guess that means they're hitting the target audience. (And hopefully you feel a little bit sophisticated reading about it in a book this time.) But despite *knowing* that too much social media harms our mental health, most of us still can't quit the habit, and we struggle to apply better "digital hygiene" to our lives.

Why can't we stop? Similar to other sins, the negative consequences of social media overuse are subtle and build over time. If I touch a hot stove, I get burned immediately and take greater care to avoid touching hot stoves in the future. Social media is less like directly touching a hot burner and more like being the frog in the pot of slowly heating water.*

One scroll through Instagram won't cause me to hate my life. But a few months of daily seeing the milestones, accomplishments, and blissful perfection in the lives of everyone I've ever made eye contact with, I start feeling a little bummed about my own circumstances. After years of watching *everyone* except me get amazing career opportunities, *everyone* except me get married, *everyone* except me capture the perfect family portrait in a wildflower field, I begin questioning whether I'm living a worthwhile life at all. I must be doing something very wrong if everyone's moving forward except for

---

*   In case you haven't heard this bizarre myth before: Amphibians can (supposedly) only feel extreme temperatures, so if you put a frog in a pot of boiling water, it'll jump out. But if you put a frog in a pot of room-temperature water and gradually turn up the heat, the frog won't notice the temperature increase and will stay in the water until it boils to death.

me! This discontentment happens even though *I logically know* negatives aren't shown and I'm only seeing the well-curated highlights.

Healthier Digital Habits

There's certainly a time and a place for memes, videos, online conversation, and scrolling to catch up with what's going on in the lives of our friends, but we need to call most of our social media use what it is: a giant time waster. If we're going to honor God with our limited time here on earth, we need to figure out a way to break social media's hold and better spend our days. "Look carefully then how you walk, not as unwise but as wise, making the best use of the time, because the days are evil" (Ephesians 5:15–16). Many of us miss opportunities to push back daily evils because we're hypnotized by our screens.

So how do we mitigate the impact of these sites? Social media is a major part of today's culture, and unless we're hit with a massive electromagnetic pulse, it's here to stay. (After the roller coaster ride of 2020, I'm not discounting anything as a possibility.) I've met a handful of people who refuse to participate in any sort of social media. (My response to them is always: "What's it like to be happy?") But for most of us, it's a daily struggle to draw a line in the digital sand.

Of the numerous approaches to handling social media overuse, the keys seem to lie in exercising moderation, intentionality, and being aware of what it reveals about our hearts.

Moderation

Controlling our amount of technology use sounds simple, but it takes incredible self-discipline and willpower. Many social media apps were designed to draw us back for more by utilizing the same kind of technology that hooks gambling addicts on slot machines in Vegas.[7] The best way for a gambling addict to avoid gambling is to stay away from casinos, and the best way for us to break our phone habits is to create some physical distance.

I've found that if my phone is near me, I will tap it. If I tap it, I will unlock it. If I unlock it, I will lose at least twenty minutes of my day. So I've learned that putting my phone out of sight for a while curbs idle checking. Unless I need it close to catch an expected call or text, I try to leave my phone in another room when I'm going about my daily business.

I've learned small adjustments go a long way when separating from my phone. I'll go for a short walk without it or lock it in my car for a while after returning from running errands. (I don't like going all the way outside to where my car is parked, so my physical laziness actually helps me be disciplined in this case.) My sleep improves considerably when I consistently turn off my phone or don't leave it by my bed at night. (Fortunately, many stores sell these things called "alarm clocks" that will wake you up at the time of your choosing.) Turning off notifications, taking Facebook completely off my phone, and logging out of apps so I'm forced to inconvenience myself with passwords each time I try to access them help me control the amount of time I spend in the digital universe.

When I first started putting distance between me and my phone, I'd get separation anxiety and often go check it. My brain had to be retrained to occupy itself when I couldn't default to my screen. After a little while, though, I remembered how to be productive and operate without my phone constantly in hand. Many of us feel exposed, vulnerable, and lost unless we're constantly checking the internet, but it's healthy to remember there's a vibrant world outside our screens.

Intentionality

Here's the tricky part about separating from our phones: The geniuses in Silicon Valley made it so our phones carry everything we need in the same place as everything we don't really need. If we use our device for email, work, research, directions, or in case of emergencies, it's hard to create distance for long.

Because of my phone's addictive properties and my personal ADD, I'll often go to do something necessary on my phone and then get sidetracked and totally forget why I picked it up in the first place. If this is you, try going online with a purpose and decide *why* you're picking up your phone before you even touch it.[8] If you're going to answer a text, say out loud (or in your head) "I'm responding to texts" or "I'm answering emails." The goal is to do what you need to do without going down a hundred time-eating rabbit trails.

If possible, work on something other than your phone. I've found that when I'm on my computer, I'm not as tempted to mindlessly click around. I can get texts, calls, and emails all through my laptop. So when I put my phone away and work on my computer, I can still be accessible without excess temptations.

Heart Awareness

Social media can be both a blessing and a curse. While we tend to hear more about its negatives, many elements of social networking can positively enhance our lives. When managed well, it connects us to others, challenges us to think, brings a little levity to life, and keeps us informed. Very often a timely verse, saying, or story someone shares encourages me uniquely in that moment. I get to stay in touch with friends and family, and I'm able to share and market my work completely free through many platforms. Likewise, I've been introduced to new comedians, restaurants, musicians, and books through my friends' posts. My life is richer in many ways because of the exposure to a broader world through social media, especially if I'm able to take what I see online and apply it in "real" life. When something I learn online motivates true heart change and transforms the way I live, then social media can play a part in my effort to push back daily evils.

It's possible to glorify God with our screen time, but it starts with understanding the deeper soul issues at the center of how we use our devices. If we pay attention, God can use our screens to reveal areas of our hearts in need of refining.

A couple of years ago, while scrolling through Facebook, I found myself feeling jealous of some of my comedian friends' successes and opportunities that weren't being given to me. My first instinct was to blame social media for causing my envy, but I would've been just as jealous had they told me in person. Facebook didn't cause my jealousy; it merely exposed it.

When God uses something to reveal our sin, we should see it as a blessing. It might not be a fun blessing, but it's a blessing nonetheless. We know that He disciplines and corrects us because He loves us (Hebrews 12:6).

Facebook didn't cause my jealousy; it merely exposed it. When God uses something to reveal our sin, we should see it as a blessing.

So as we take measures to remove ourselves from the addictive grasp of social media, we should pay attention to the heart struggles it's revealing. We can start by asking ourselves some basic questions: Why do we feel the need to post about every single thing we do? What will we really miss if we don't log on for a day? What does our online life allow us to avoid in real life? Does what we're seeing online bring us envy, joy, or another reaction? Does it drive us to action or anxiety? Does the way we're using social media enrich our "real" life or damage it?

As we seek to develop healthy, God-honoring digital habits, we can, as my friend Arlene Pellicane puts it, "use technology without letting it use us."[9]

Considerations

1. What social media platforms do you use, and how much time do you spend on them each day?

2. What does your social media use reveal about your heart? What are the motives behind what you post and check?

3. How can you "push back daily evils" through your social media use?

A Little Bit Extra

It may be helpful to create a mission statement for positive social media use. I decided a few years back that I would use social media to share laughter and encouragement, promote my comedy, and stay updated with my family and friends. Having this mind-set keeps me from getting pulled into angry comment threads and venting, and it helps me decide when and what to block.

CHAPTER 9

Friendship Is the Best Ship

"Kindred spirits are not so scarce as I used to think."

Anne Shirley, *Anne of Green Gables*

When I turned seven, my family moved to a new neighborhood. Shortly after settling into our new home, my mom took me and my siblings to a nearby park. There, while running up and down the slides, I met Jenny. I think "barreled into Jenny" might be more accurate since I collided into her while going down a slide she was attempting to walk up. Jenny and I bonded instantly. By the end of park time, we'd declared ourselves best friends, and to our great fortune, we discovered our families lived just a few houses away from each other. Jenny and I saw each other almost every day until we were teenagers, when my family moved again.

I often wish I could simply go down a slide every time I needed a friend, but the truth is both friendships and going down slides become more challenging with age.

Right now, one of the ongoing epidemics facing Western civilization is loneliness. According to a recent survey, two out of ten Americans feel chronically lonely.[1] Another study shows an even more drastic picture: nearly half of all Americans feel always or sometimes lonely.[2] Even hospitality industries are noticing this new wave of isolation, as reservations for dining alone have gone up 62 percent since 2014.[3] (From personal experience, dining by yourself is enjoyable and relaxing unless someone you know walks in and sees you eating alone. Then it becomes lame and embarrassing.)

We all long to find our "tribe," but work, responsibilities, and the ease with which we can create and maintain relationships online make connecting with people in person difficult. Building friendships and community in a society where seclusion is the norm[4] takes a mix of work, patience, and God's divine blessing. Is it possible?

The Dance of Friendship

In an earlier chapter I brought up that, as a single woman in my midthirties, I'm accustomed to being asked, "Well, are you putting yourself out there?" Because I *know* how frustrating that question can be, it's with much hypocritical awareness that I pose to you the same question about friendships: "Are you putting yourself out there?"

Let me assure you, relationships of any kind require extra energy when you're of adulting age. So, if you find yourself frustrated by the effort it takes to make friends at this stage, you're not alone. Because we're generally so busy and geographically spread out, friendships require prioritizing face-to-face interaction and physically *going* to places where other people will be. (And then not hiding behind our phones once we get there.)

Besides the actual effort of showing up, making friends requires openness and vulnerability. It's pretty much the same rules as when we were kids, except as full-fledged adults we're more aware of the risk and awkwardness inherent in human interaction. This is why social media friendships are so appealing: we can minimize or eliminate much of the risk from behind a screen. (And if you *do* end up not getting along with someone, technology makes it much easier to uninvite the person from your birthday party. As kids we had to say it to the other kid's face; now we can covertly remove someone's email from the Evite.) As author Tony Reinke put it, "Hiding our unflattering features is very natural and easy online, but excruciatingly hard and unnatural offline, in healthy local churches, and honest friendships."[5]

Unfortunately, without taking these risks there is very little reward. Many of us are settling for something much less than what God offers us through "real" friendships, especially with fellow believers. Proverbs tells us, "As iron sharpens iron, so one person sharpens another" (Proverbs 27:17 NIV). Iron isn't sharpened by sitting comfortably in a case; it's sharpened by being heated, struck, and filed by other instruments. Good, life-giving friendships challenge us to grow and mature as humans and followers of Christ.

When you read through the Bible, it's evident that we're meant to go through life with other Christians. God even models fellowship for us through the Trinity—the Father, Son, and Holy Spirit dwelling together in perfect community. When Jesus came to earth, He surrounded Himself with a group of friends. Though Jesus was relationally complete as God, He was also fully man, and the human part of Him desired and valued close community.

Fellow believers are so important to one another that the Bible refers to those who are in Christ as being members of the same body (1 Corinthians 12:12). Sometimes a strong spiritual community can feel more like family than our own biological relatives.

Many of us are settling for something much less than what God offers us through "real" friendships, especially with fellow believers.

Maybe you've heard the phrase "blood is thicker than water." That saying has gone through numerous iterations over the years, but one of the earliest versions reads: "The blood of the covenant is thicker than the water of the womb."[6] Basically, people who share in a promise have a deeper connection than a mother has with her child. The people who share in the promises of God will be closer to us than a nonbelieving family member. God, in His divine mercy, sets the lonely in families (Psalm 68:6), and often that's played out through the body of Christ.

I've been fortunate to experience deep and meaningful friendships with people who took the time to get to know me and invite me to be part of their lives. They've included me in game nights, added a seat at their table during family dinners, and one year a family from my church dropped by my house at the last minute to see if I wanted to go see Christmas lights with them. (Heck yes I did!) These simple gestures gave me a profound sense of belonging, but I had to do my part too. Over and over I've had to step out, show up, and give people the opportunity to include me.

Many of these friendships were formed through attending a local church. Sometimes I was brave enough to overpower awkwardness and connect with the people sitting around me during the meet-and-greet time. Other times I bonded with people through volunteering and serving. My community also grew through official church-organized small groups. Almost always, though, the beginning stages of these relationships took a little bit of work, required leaving my comfort zone, and made me open myself up to the ups and downs of living life alongside other sinners who are also doing their best.

The Patience of Friendship

We all want authenticity in our relationships, but reliable friendships don't happen at the snap of our fingers. Most friendships need to start with transparency, which means being open and not hiding. Then gradually, as trust builds, they transition to vulnerability, which is a deeper, even more sacred connection.[7] True relationship develops over time as we learn to embrace the messy, unpolished people God has put around us.

We're so accustomed to the immediate "friendships" we form online that if we don't instantly bond with someone in person, we write it off as "not clicking" and give up. We forget that getting to know someone takes time and patience. Online friendships can be built in seconds, with the tap of a screen. With a few exceptions, deep, godly friendships can take months and years to build over awkward conversations, casual meals, and sheepish requests for a ride to the airport during rush hour. They happen through perseverance and understanding the bigger picture: these are the souls we're going to "do life" with here on earth and then see for all eternity!

The Divine Blessing of Friendship

Not long ago, while driving through Texas for some shows, I stopped to visit the grown daughter of longtime family friends. She had married a year prior, then moved after the wedding to a new city, and now she had just given birth to her first child. (That's a lot of change for one year.)

We chatted a little bit, and she expressed to me the deep loneliness she felt in her new life. She'd thought marriage and motherhood would safeguard her from this kind of isolation, but she found herself longing for good friendships more than ever.

Unfortunately, despite her efforts to get involved in a local church, she hadn't formed any friendships or developed much in the way of community. Everywhere she went, it seemed, people were busy with their own lives and already had full social cups. There didn't seem to be any more room for her.

I call this a friendship drought. We think exclusion from the "cool table" ends after high school, but unfortunately, it's often part of adulting too. Sometimes even when we do all the "right" things, community just doesn't seem to happen. At some point in life, despite your efforts, you too may experience a season like this.

My first friendship drought happened during my college years. I longed for deep community and did everything necessary on the "make friends" checklist. I went to college ministry gatherings. I joined clubs. I participated in study groups. At the end of the day, though, I didn't have a single non-family person I could reach out to if I needed anything. I knew people in a surface-level way, but no deeper than that. Everything I tried had an atmosphere of superficiality, even the church groups. No one sought to include me outside the parameters of whatever meeting I attended, and sometimes I even sensed that my presence inconvenienced everyone, since a new person can throw off the dynamics of an already-established group.

No matter our age, status, or life stage, feeling like we're on the outside hurts (especially when we hop onto Snapchat and see everyone else seeming to live out their best lives with a group of besties). In the Old Testament, we're told the story of Job. God permitted Satan to take everything from him (Job 1–2). Amid the death of his children, watching all his material possessions literally go up in smoke, and then getting struck with disease, one of Job's laments, oddly enough, was his lack of good friends. "My friends scorn me; my eye pours out tears to God" (Job 16:20).

Unfortunately, friendships might not happen during some seasons. Your adulting responsibilities may get in the way of building or maintaining friendships, or people you've come to count on may simply abandon you or let you down due to their own circumstances.

Don't lose hope. Separation from people doesn't mean separation from God. If you're feeling lonely and on the outside of things, take it before Jesus, who understands what it's like to be on the fringes of society

(Isaiah 53:3). View this as a season to grow closer to your truest Friend, and continue asking God, the giver of all good things, to bring you good community. It's a prayer request He's answered for me numerous times.

Before my most recent move from Colorado Springs to Atlanta, I prayed that God would bring me meaningful friendships in my new city. God didn't immediately answer my prayer for friendship, but a few months into living in Atlanta I met Tracie. She introduced herself to me during our megachurch's meet-and-greet time, and we quickly discovered that we lived in the same neighborhood. (Was this the adulting version of going down a slide?!) She invited me to join her family at our community pool that afternoon, where we got to know each other a little bit more. Later she introduced me to a few of our other neighbors, and over the next couple of years I grew close to several families in the neighborhood. We walked with each other through difficult seasons of death, illness, and other hardships.

One evening, as I walked back down the road to my home after spending the afternoon at a neighbor's house, it occurred to me that these friendships were an answer to the prayer I had prayed before leaving Colorado. In a church of five thousand-plus people, spanning multiple services and worship locations, the chances of me sitting next to a woman who lived one street over were minuscule. (And given the insulated nature of our suburban neighborhood, Tracie and I might never have met otherwise.) But God heard and answered my prayer for good friends. I didn't have a huge community, but the friends God gave me were the ones I needed in that season. (And they continue to be great friends, even though I've since moved to a different neighborhood.)

A Shift in Perspective

If the statistics about lonely people are true, there are plenty of opportunities for friendship; they just need to be found. Rather than viewing friendship as something you *get*, start thinking of it as something you *give*. This isn't a license to let people constantly walk all over us; it simply shifts the focus off ourselves and allows us to see people who might need to experience the love of Jesus through friendship.

---

*Rather than viewing friendship as something you **get**, start thinking of it as something you **give**.*

It can be hard and awkward, especially for those on the more introverted side, but pray and ask God to provide a genuine love and interest for other people. This others-centered perspective allows space for friendships to grow and thrive.

Be willing to take the plunge and initiate the conversation with someone if you're in a new setting. It's easy to hold back and hope other people will reach out to *you*, especially if you're the new kid on the block, but there's a good chance that everyone around you is just as nervous and waiting on someone else to break the tension.

In other words, we should be friendly. Friendliness is a practical way of loving our neighbors as ourselves. Jesus came to earth and faced rejection, hardship, and sacrificed His own life to be a friend to sinners. As His followers, we can step out of our comfort zone and offer friendship, even if it starts out a little clunky and awkward. (And if that makes you anxious, the next chapter is just for you.)

Considerations

1. Where are you at with friendships and godly community? Are you satisfied with your meaningful relationships? Or lacking in them?

2. Why do you think friendships are so much harder to build and maintain as adults?

3. How can you "give friendship" to those around you?

A Little Bit Extra

Godly community isn't always going to look picture perfect. Our natural tendency is to surround ourselves with people whose lives look like our own. It's wonderful to have people around you who are in the same life stage and experiencing similar struggles, but there's value in spending time with believers of all ages and backgrounds. Some of my most life-giving friendships are with people who aren't my age, aren't in my same life stage, and with whom I share very little in common outside of Jesus.

CHAPTER 10

Cue the Anxiety

"I've had a lot of worries in my life, most of which never happened."
Mark Twain

One time, when I was a child, I was allowed to watch a news special on plane crashes. (Please keep in mind I still was not allowed to watch *Barney* or *The Smurfs*.) Shortly after viewing the program and its horrifying images and stories, I traveled on a flight that experienced severe turbulence. As you can probably understand, I consequently developed a fear of flying that stayed with me well into adulthood. Over the years, numerous people attempted to help rid me of my flying anxiety. Many pointed out that, statistically speaking, I was way safer in a plane than in a car. (This only made me afraid of the drive to the airport.) My pilot father drew diagrams of how planes and choppy air worked, thinking knowledge might bring me peace of mind. Another friend showed me an app that charted out where a flight might experience turbulence due to weather, believing I'd settle down if I simply knew what to expect. No matter what anyone said, I'd spend the days leading up to a flight stressing out, which isn't good when you fly every few days for your job.

The most extreme intervention came from two of my younger siblings. One year my younger brother and youngest sister, both certified skydivers, decided to take me skydiving as a birthday gift. I agreed to go *only* because my brother assured me that skydiving would cure me once and for all of my fear of flying, and probably all my other fears too. (He also said they would mock me the rest of my life for being a chicken if I didn't accept their generous gift. Siblings are the best.)

My brother and sister both planned to join me, but unfortunately a few days before the Big Day, my sister broke her foot while—you're never going to believe it—skydiving! Because of her injury, she could no longer go with us. My brother, however, promised he would be with me right up until we jumped out of the plane. He would jump solo, while I jumped tandem. If you're unfamiliar with tandem skydiving, it's an option that allows complete amateurs to experience the joys of plummeting to the ground at 120 miles per hour without having to first complete any training. Basically, I'd have a professional skydiver strapped to my back doing all the work, leaving me completely free to focus on not having a heart attack.

Our first attempt to skydive was thwarted by a thunderstorm (prayer works!), but we returned to the center a few days later to complete the mission. After signing away my right to sue anyone if I died, I was shown a brief safety video; then the man who was to be my human backpack for the afternoon began fitting me for equipment.

To make a long story short, I hated every single moment of my skydiving experience. From cramming into the back of a plane that looked like Chitty Chitty Bang Bang, to standing on the edge of the plane looking at the miles-away earth, to finally gliding down in the parachute, I wanted to bail the entire time. (Unfortunately, once out of the plane you're pretty much committed to seeing it through.) My family, who'd come for moral support (and probably for the potential comedy), offered me their sincerest congratulations on completing my first skydive. My brother, as it turned out, was certain I was going to change my mind at altitude and be a "fail to jump," the lowest and most humiliating of labels to be stuck with in the skydiving world. If nothing else, at least the experience gave me the satisfaction of proving him wrong.

"But at least you're probably not afraid of flying anymore!" he said after debriefing me.

"I'm actually even *more* afraid of flying," I told him. "Because I now know how terrible it is to free-fall."

He laughed and told me I was the only person he'd heard of who went skydiving and came out with *more* fears. It's a badge I wear proudly.

I've referenced fear and anxiety throughout this book, and I went back and forth about whether to devote an entire chapter to the topic. However, I've met countless people dealing with it on some level, and surveys have shown that 30 percent of younger adults experience anxiety severe enough to disrupt their workdays.[1] I want to share a few tools and insights I've found helpful in battling my own anxiety over the years, in the hopes that they'll bring some relief to your own worries and fears* (and, Lord willing, not make them worse).

Over the years, I've noticed my anxieties generally fall into one of two categories: practical and soul.

Practical Anxiety

As I transitioned into college and then my early twenties, much of my anxiety came from wondering if I was equipped to handle everything I'd encounter in life. Growing up, my parents took care of most day-to-day responsibilities so I could focus on my school and my extracurricular activities.

While older generations were forced to be self-sufficient at an earlier age, many in younger generations have been pushed to concentrate on school, excel in sports or other activities, and be well-rounded individuals so they can get into a good university. Our job wasn't to have life figured out; it was to be excellent students. Even high schools took away courses like home economics and consumer sciences/personal finances to make way for classes that would better prepare students for collegiate testing.[2]

The intention was to give us an edge when we entered the workforce as college graduates, but the result has been a generation of ill-prepared adults who don't know how to make a budget, fill a prescription, or do laundry. I remember the mild shock I experienced when I moved out on my own and learned that postage stamps didn't

---

*   You've probably already picked up on the fact that I'm using *worry*, *fear*, and *anxiety* interchangeably. As a writer, I don't want to use the word *anxiety* four hundred times in one chapter, so I'm mixing it up with a few of Webster's suggested synonyms.

automatically materialize in my desk's top drawer. As it turned out, someone had to buy them and put them there. (Growing up, that someone was my dad.)

The *good* news about practical anxiety is that life eventually forces you to learn things as you need them. The *bad* news is that you actually have to step up and figure out how to do these things, and that can be scary at first.

When I moved to Los Angeles in my early twenties, I'd never made my own doctor's appointment or dealt with health insurance. My mom had always done all that for me. When I came down with a nasty upper respiratory and sinus infection about a year into living in LA, I was forced to research doctors, make an appointment, figure out what my insurance covered, and pay the remaining bill. Did I call my mom crying in a panic four times? Absolutely. Did I get laughed at by an insurance agent for asking what a copay was? You bet. But did I successfully find a doctor, pick up my prescription, and get rid of my sinus infection? I sure did! One of the mysteries of adulting had come into the light, and a little part of my anxiety disappeared.

A similar thing happened when my car broke down one night in Los Angeles. After freaking out and wishing I had joined the Amish instead of moving to an unfamiliar city, I texted a friend to come get me, called my dad to inquire how one went about getting a tow truck, received a referral for a mechanic, and got my car fixed.

Mastering basic adulting skills by myself gave me confidence that I'd also be able to figure out the next problem. While practical anxieties still plague me from time to time, they've calmed down a lot with age and experience.

As you encounter practical anxieties, remember it's normal to feel nervous or unsure when facing new situations. If you're feeling incredibly stressed, take a moment to pray and ask God to help you through your circumstances. I promise He cares about even your most trivial adulting woes.

As you encounter practical anxieties, remember it's normal to feel nervous or unsure when facing new situations.

Then, call your parents, do an online search, or reach out to someone more experienced to get started on the first steps. Pro tip: Let people help you, but avoid allowing someone to completely take over solving the problem for you. It may make you feel less stressed in the moment, but it won't reduce your anxieties in the long term.

Soul Anxiety

While practical anxieties often come from a lack of knowledge or experience, soul anxieties are a bit more abstract—such as that feeling of unease we sometimes get upon realizing we don't control the world and everything in it. Soul anxieties tend to whisper a very destructive lie: God will allow the worst to happen and then split.

I first began experiencing soul anxiety during my college years. I'd look ahead at the blank pages of my life and imagine them filled with a series of worst-case scenarios. (It also doesn't help that, as we get older, we become more aware of all the things that *can* go wrong and then fear they'll happen to us.) I think most people experience soul anxieties at some point, but some seem more sensitive to them than others.

Though soul anxieties still show up unannounced sometimes, I've gotten better at recognizing them and tackling them head-on when they surface. (The trick mentioned in chapter 3 about knowing and speaking truth to yourself when feelings fail can also be applied to dealing with anxiety.)

Fighting the Good Fight

Through the years, I've heard varying arguments about the root of anxiety. Some people argue that anxiety is a sin and to be anxious disobeys Jesus' command not to worry (Matthew 6:25–34). Others say it's an affliction outside our control, meant to point us back to the grace of God. I fall more into the "anxiety as an affliction" camp, but I also don't believe we're meant to helplessly drown in it our entire lives. I think God gives us both the means and the opportunity to transform our greatest fears and worries into trust and faith.

The problem is that moving from "fear and worry" to "trust and faith" isn't as simple as flipping a switch. (Although, admittedly, my anxiety eases quite a bit when I'm not flipping my coffeemaker's switch from "off" to "brew" fourteen times a day.) God commands us to take every thought captive (2 Corinthians 10:5), and that includes the ones driving us to fear and worry. A useful exercise I've found for taking my anxious thoughts captive comes from Bible teacher and speaker Beth Moore.

Moore suggests grabbing hold of an anxiety spiral by asking yourself "Then what?" when fear starts to creep in.[3] Say your house burns down. *Then what?* You get a hotel while it gets repaired. *Then what?* Insurance decides the reason it burned down isn't covered in your policy. *Then what?* You live in a cheap apartment for a while until you can rebuild your savings. And so on, and so on. As you take your thoughts captive by considering the potential outcomes of worst-case scenarios, you'll begin to see that you can handle even the most far-fetched catastrophes. Plus, remember that no circumstance, no matter how terrible, will ever separate you from the love of Christ.

Incidentally, I had to do the "then what?" exercise when I got the contract to write this book. I had earnestly prayed that God would allow my book proposal to be picked up by a publisher. As soon as that happened, though, my anxiety launched into overdrive. What if I finished the manuscript and the publishers hated it and pulled the plug? What if a few months before the release date, someone else published a book with my exact same title and concept? What if I somehow broke all my fingers and couldn't type? (This one is admittedly ridiculous, but it did cross my mind.) What if the night before my deadline my computer crashed and erased all my work, and all three of my backup hard drives *and* my cloud account got wiped too? What if the book received scathing reviews and I got lots of Christian hate mail? What if?! What if?! What if?!

My wheels spun out of control to the point where I almost returned the advance and canceled the contract. Fortunately (and I hope you think it's fortunate as well), I caught myself and started, one by one, submitting my fears about the project to God.

What if the publishers hate it?
Then I'd either return the advance or rewrite it. It might hurt my ego, but I'd survive.

What if someone happened to write the exact same book as me, title and everything?
Then I'd return the advance and start working on another book or change the title. Or I'd cut my losses as a writer and refocus my efforts on becoming an accordion-playing clown for Cirque du Soleil.

What if I broke all my fingers and couldn't type?
We're in the twenty-first century. There is now talk-to-text software. In fact, I think a better question is, "Why am I typing at all?"

What if five forms of digital backup failed?
Then clearly this book was not meant to be. (Or I was sabotaged—in which case, I've always wanted to solve a mystery!)

What if people hated it and wrote nasty reviews and sent mean messages to me?

This was probably the only anxiety rooted in a bit of reality, as people aren't always kind when they don't like someone's work. But even this outcome would probably teach me a lot of important lessons about humility and resiliency. (And perhaps it would provide sufficient motivation to stay off the internet for a spell.)

For God has not given us a spirit of fear, but of power and of love and of sound mind. (2 Timothy 1:7 NKJV)

This leads me to the second tool I've found helpful in curbing anxiety: reminding myself early and often that if I let fear call the shots, I'll miss out on seeing God work through me. After passing up an opportunity to travel as a teenager because I was scared to get on the plane, I decided that I would never again miss doing something because I was scared to fly. (I'm still impressed teenage me made that decision.)

If I let fear call the shots, I'll miss out on seeing God work through me.

Though my writing fears weren't flying related, I realized my anxieties were once again trying to dictate my life. After working through them, I was forced to acknowledge this: God, against all twenty-first-century publishing odds, gave me, a relatively unknown author and comedian, the chance to write a book and have it published. I could withdraw out of fear and definitely miss seeing how He could use my work, or I could trust Him with the unknowns and have faith that He would use this experience—whether a dream or a nightmare—for my good and His glory.

Anxiety and God's Tender Care

The absolute best antidote for anxiety is remembering God's ever-present love and faithfulness. If you're like me, however, you probably have a very short memory. Numerous times in my life God has miraculously provided for me, not just financially and materially, but also spiritually and emotionally. And yet within days (sometimes even hours) of His provision, I'd already be worrying about my next problem and doubting whether He cared about it.

Several years ago, I was challenged to start journaling my prayers. I wrote down all my wants, needs, and worries into a notebook. Then, every few months I'd go back through old entries and jot down how each situation had resolved. It was incredible to see a written record of God's faithfulness in matters both big and small. He even answered prayers I'd completely forgotten about praying. Over time, I saw that even God's "no" answers had been in my best interest, which helped me trust the "no" and "not yet" answers I didn't understand.

In January of 2018, my younger brother Mark (the one who took me skydiving at the beginning of the chapter) deployed to

Iraq with his Air Force Pararescue unit. Shortly after he left for his deployment, I wrote in my prayer journal, "Protection for Mark."

In March of 2018, less than two months into his deployment, Mark was killed in a helicopter crash while on a night mission with his team. It was the most gut-wrenching "no" I'd ever received from God in response to a prayer.

While processing through the blender of grief and sadness that came with Mark's sudden and traumatic death, it occurred to me that I hadn't told him how proud I was of him. At least, not that I could remember.

I had a great relationship with my brother, and while I assumed he probably knew that I was proud of him, grief isn't always a rational creature. I'd lie in bed at night wishing I could turn back the clock and send him a text or call him up and leave a voice mail letting him know how proud I was of the man he'd become.

A couple of months after Mark died, my older sister informed me that she'd been sorting through the belongings he'd left stored at her house and found some letters and cards I'd sent to him a decade earlier when he was going through basic training at the Air Force Academy. In an ultimate return-to-sender, I received them back.

I read through each note, unable to control my tears. At the bottom of a postcard I'd sent him, I had written in all caps, "I AM EXTREMELY PROUD OF YOU." My brother kept everything I'd sent him all those years ago. I unexpectedly had assurance that he'd known what I longed to tell him.

This discovery came with another revelation: God truly cares about the smallest details of our lives, even in, perhaps *especially* in, our suffering. Whenever I start to question whether God cares about the details of my life, I look at that postcard.

I didn't know when I wrote those letters that they'd be brought back to comfort me during one of life's darkest moments. But God knew. When I wrote to my brother during his basic training, the Lord was already preparing my heart for what was coming ten years down the road. God took what was *known* in that moment—that my brother needed encouragement during his grueling training—and tucked it away for what was *unknown* at that time—that my only brother would be brought Home early, and the letters would come back as a source of consolation to me. And while I'd had earthly protection in mind when I wrote my prayer request for my brother's protection, I realized Mark was permanently safe and eternally alive in the presence of his Savior. In a grander sense, God had answered "yes" to my request for Mark's safety.

Moving Forward

A few years ago, it occurred to me that I no longer feared flying. I can't pinpoint exactly when my airborne anxiety went away, but at some point, it did. Though I'll probably never enjoy flying through turbulence, it was refreshing to realize that my seemingly immovable fear had vanished. Maybe I finally flew enough times to get over it, maybe my skydive actually helped in the long run, or maybe I just realized that if I died in a plane crash, I wouldn't have to worry about whether my hypothetical kids understood math or whether I had enough money saved for retirement. Whatever the reason, it gave me hope that the rest of my fears and anxieties would eventually go away.

Though the phrase "do not fear" is found 365 times throughout the Bible, Jesus never gave platitudes like "that won't happen" or "just stop thinking about it" to His followers when helping them deal with anxiety. He simply reminded them that He cared for them deeply and that through Him was a beautiful alternative to daily worry: trust. Jesus promises to be with us every step of our journey, carrying our burdens and preparing our tomorrow so we can focus on our today (1 Peter 5:7; Matthew 11:28–30).

God, who knows the end from the beginning (Isaiah 46:10), is gently preparing you *now* for what you'll walk through in the *future*. As Corrie ten Boom eloquently put it, "Never be afraid to trust an unknown future to a known God."

Considerations

1. What are some of your fears, worries, and anxieties? How do you currently handle them?

2. Why do you think Jesus commands us not to worry (Matthew 6:25–34), knowing it's something that can be hard to control?

3. Do you think it's possible to have complete peace in the midst of an ever-changing, increasingly volatile world?

A Little Bit Extra

If *God is good (Psalm 34:8), keeps His promises (2 Corinthians 1:20), ordains all that happens to maximize His glory and our joy (Isaiah*

48:9–11; John 15:11), sees and knows all (Job 28:24), acts only for our good (Romans 8:28), is preparing a reward so great that our present sorrows aren't worthy of being compared to it (Romans 8:18), has perfect timing (Habakkuk 2:3), and won't let anything separate us from His love (Romans 8:38–39), then *He is worthy of trust—the kind of trust that drives out fear, worry, and anxiety.*

CHAPTER 11

Operation Expectation Adjustment

"Blessed is he who expects nothing, for he shall never be disappointed."
Alexander Pope

For the past couple of years, I've pretty much made my living through comedy and writing. While the creative aspect of working as an artist is rewarding, "living the dream" looks nothing like the glamour and excitement I imagined. It often manifests as a string of hotels, early morning flights, and lukewarm airport food. It's time away from family and friends, little financial stability, and being in a city without ever seeing the city. To put it in a way that sets up this chapter: it's not at all what I expected.

My guess is that certain, perhaps even all, aspects of life haven't met your expectations. One of the greatest frustrations I hear about "adulting" is that so many of our hopes and dreams end up as disappointments.

Over and over I've heard (and said) things like:

"I figured I'd be married by now and not having to make all these huge decisions alone."

"I thought I'd be financially secure by this point."

"I joined the group thinking it would be a good way to get to know some people, but no one even talks to me."

"I expected this test to be easier to pass."

"I expected to get over this loss quicker."

"I expected marriage to be more satisfying."

"I expected to have at least a couple of kids by my age."

"I expected to have this all figured out by now."

I've decided that adulting, when boiled down to its essence, consists largely of adjusting our expectations and looking for a pen (and then looking for a different pen when the first one you find is unexpectedly out of ink).

Are we supposed to abandon all our hopes, dreams, and expectations merely to eliminate the risk of disappointment? How do we harness our expectations to be glorifying to God and stimulate joy instead of discouragement?

Disappointment Management

Each one of us operates with expectations that are both small and large, immediate and long-term, realistic and unrealistic.

Realistic expectations are shaped by experience and what we're taught.[1] We expect the sun to rise in the morning (unless we live very far north or south during certain times of the year) because it has risen every day in the past. We look both ways before crossing the street because we've been taught to expect cars on the road. We go to Chipotle because, from experience, we can expect to get a decent burrito for $8.

Unrealistic expectations happen when your heart gets set on a certain result that you have limited control over attaining. You expect a friend to return the favor when you go out of your way to help him or her. You expect to be promoted in your job by a certain time. You expect your European vacation to provide a lifetime of perfect memories, but you end up bed-bound with the flu the entire trip.

If you're able to catch your unrealistic expectations and adjust them, do it! Sometimes, though, we don't even realize we've been holding on to expectations until a situation goes a certain way and we suddenly find ourselves upset and disappointed.

One expert suggests the first unrealistic expectation we can have is believing we can completely eliminate all unrealistic expectations.[2]

Disappointment, which is the by-product of unmet expectations, is a natural part of living in a fallen world. It's unrealistic to think life can be totally absent of it. It's our response to disappointment that matters. If we're not careful, unmet expectations can create the perfect conditions for bitterness, self-pity, and cynicism to grow in our hearts.

When I left Los Angeles, having failed at my dream of comedy writing, I said, "Okay, fine, God. Since You obviously don't care about my heart's desires, do whatever You want with my life."

This clearly wasn't joyful submission to God's will. This was a thinly veiled attempt to pass off bitterness and cynicism as holy surrender when life didn't go the way I expected. Cynicism is an especially destructive mind-set that says, "I'm not even going to bother hoping because nothing ever works out for me anyway." Though we attempt to use it as a way of protecting ourselves from further hurt, cynicism destroys joy faster than a gas-station burrito destroys the digestive system.

Instead of growing cynical, the apostle Paul offers us a different approach to handling life's curveballs: "Rejoice in hope, be patient in tribulation, be constant in prayer" (Romans 12:12). Instead of giving ourselves over to self-pity and despair, we're to fill the emptiness left by unmet expectations with hope, patience, and prayer.

We're *meant* to care about the dreams and desires God has placed on our hearts, but we're also meant to trust our heavenly Father *above* those dreams and desires. Our hope must always be placed in God's will being done, even after we realize that His plan is probably going to be different from the one we wanted Him to sign off on.

I learned a lot from my friend Amelia about placing my hope in God's ultimate plan. Amelia was born premature and grew up with cerebral palsy, a condition that affected her balance and muscular control, requiring her to be in a wheelchair or walk with a special set of crutches.

But Amelia's physical handicaps didn't slow her down in the slightest. She worked as a comedy manager (we met when she was managing a comedian that I opened for at the time) and traveled all over the country both for her job and for fun.

Amelia had a huge heart for people and always wanted to be a missionary to Africa. She believed God was using her disability to uniquely prepare her for an international calling. At the time, I was considering a move to South America to teach, so Amelia and I shared our excitement over how God might use us in our respective fields of ministry.

And then, Amelia's cerebral palsy began causing serious health complications. After going in for a surgery to help alleviate some pain she'd been having in her stomach, Amelia became fully bed-bound.

It became clear that, short of a miracle—which Amelia was convinced God could and would do if He so desired—she would never make it to Africa to see her missionary dreams realized. Amelia spent the last year of her life in a hospital bed set up at her childhood home.

Even in her final days, when her pain was constant and the hope of improvement was rapidly fading, Amelia never felt sorry for herself. Her positive attitude always baffled me because I've thrown full-on pity parties when I couldn't find a pair of clippers to trim a hangnail. Rather than wallow in misery or resentment, Amelia rejoiced in the hope of God using her present circumstances, despite them not being what she wanted or expected.

One day, while she and I chatted on the phone, Amelia brought up the subject of her new reality.

"I always thought I would end up overseas doing mission work," Amelia told me. "But then God showed me that this bed is supposed to be my Africa."

She knew God called her to minister to those needing the hope of Jesus. Her situation didn't change that calling, just the location of it. The hospital bed in her room became her mission field, and she had a very active ministry. People came over to check in on her but ended up leaving encouraged by her. You couldn't help but leave Amelia's bedside filled up.

Amelia passed away in the summer of 2018, and shortly after her death, her parents gave me one of the many Bibles she'd owned. As I flipped through the pages one morning, looking at some of the notes she'd scribbled and highlighted, I stopped at a verse in the Psalms she'd underlined:

> I remain confident of this:
>   I will see the goodness of the LORD
>   in the land of the living.
> Wait for the LORD;
>   be strong and take heart
>   and wait for the LORD. (Psalm 27:13–14 NIV)

Amelia had confidence of God's goodness in His promise of eternity, but she fully expected to see His goodness *this side* of eternity as well.

Though disappointments can feel all-encompassing, when we patiently wait for the Lord's plan to unfold, we see how He sustains us through every up and down. And if we're looking, we even see His goodness in our unmet expectations along the way.

Lastly, God has given us a powerful weapon in battling disappointment: prayer. We often underestimate prayer because we don't always see its effectiveness immediately, but prayer gives us the opportunity to freely and honestly talk to God about everything going on in our hearts. We can approach Him with confidence, knowing that He not only hears us but genuinely cares about every issue we bring before Him (Hebrews 4:15–16). As God listens and answers, something else subtle and incredible happens: our desires shift and start lining up with the heart of God. Through prayer, our heavenly Father performs perhaps the biggest miracle: He gives us the ability to say "Thy will be done" with joy and excitement.

Managing our expectations and disappointments with hope, patience, and prayer opens our eyes to ways God may be working outside our own plans.

God *will* turn our mourning into dancing, even if it doesn't happen right away. Our sorrow over life's unmet expectations will, at some point, give way to an eternity of joy.

Godly Expectancy

Before the onset of high-tech navigational tools, sailors used the stars to find their headings. The North Star was the most useful star because it never changed position. While other stars shifted depending on the earth's rotation, the North Star hovered (and continues to hover) over the same spot night to night, pointing to what's called "true north." Since true north never changed, sailors could find the North Star and have confidence in their direction. They might not know exactly how long it would take them to reach their destination or what they would encounter on the way, but they at least knew where they were going.

God is our True North for expectations.[3] We can expect God to be faithful to His character, to keep His promises, and to work everything for our good. We know where we're heading, but we don't know what we'll go through or how long we'll endure various seasons.

God is our True North for expectations.

God doesn't view time the same way we do as finite humans. To Him, one day is like a thousand years and a thousand years is like a day (2 Peter 3:8–9; Habakkuk 2:3). Throughout Scripture, God worked on His own timeline, often moving things along much slower than humans would prefer.

For example, in Genesis 3:15, shortly after sin entered the world, God promised a Savior to redeem humanity. And then … life went on. We see a world suffering under the influence of sin and the grief mankind's rebellion brought to God. Generations came and went without evidence of the promised Savior. Why was it taking so long for this Redeemer to come? Did God forget?

Finally, in Genesis 15, God promised a man named Abraham that he would have a son with his wife, Sarah, and through this son the entire world would be blessed (Genesis 22:18). God hadn't forgotten His promise! Both Abraham and Sarah expected a child immediately,[4] but a full ten years went by before their son Isaac was born. (Sarah, by this time, was in her nineties.) Then, thousands of years after Isaac was born, Jesus, a descendant of Abraham, blessed the whole world through His perfect life, brutal death, and supernatural resurrection.

God was faithful to keep His promise, but it certainly didn't happen quickly. In addition to following an unexpected timeline,

God's divine plan often includes surprise twists and turns that force us to acknowledge His sovereignty. As we see through the Bible, God over and over again used the unexpected to bring about the expected:

- God set apart the Israelites, a weak and uninfluential tribe by the world's standards, to be His chosen people.
- Moses, a coward and a stutterer, led God's people out of Egypt after hundreds of years of slavery (Exodus 3–12).
- David, an overlooked shepherd, became king over the Israelite kingdom of Judah (1 Samuel 17; 2 Samuel 2).
- Rahab, a prostitute who risked her life to save God's prophets, became part of the lineage of Christ (Joshua 2; Matthew 1:5).
- Ruth, a foreigner who married an Israelite, chose to stay with her mother-in-law and God's people after her husband died, and in so doing became a great-grandmother of Jesus (by several generations, Matthew 1).

Throughout the Old Testament, God used the weak, the sinful, and those on the outside to accomplish His plans.

When Jesus finally arrived, His earthly reign looked nothing like what people expected from a heavenly Redeemer. They anticipated a powerful leader who would overthrow the harsh Roman government and create a kingdom where the Israelites could finally reign peacefully and free from oppression (John 6:15).[5] Instead, Jesus came quietly and in the humblest of circumstances, born in a stable and raised in a small town that no one expected anything great to come from (John 1:46).

Instead of overthrowing rulers and establishing an earthly throne, Jesus laid down His own life to establish an eternal, heavenly kingdom. Instead of offering status and prominence to His children, He encouraged them to imitate His example and lay down their own lives and follow Him. He offered life, and life abundant, but not the kind people expected (John 10:10).

The *same* God who worked intricately throughout the Old Testament to bring about His promises, the *same* God who sent His only Son to die for our sins, is the *same* God we serve today. "The Lord is not slow to fulfill his promise as some count slowness, but is patient toward you, not wishing that any should perish, but that all should reach repentance" (2 Peter 3:9).

God still uses unexpected people to bring the hope of Jesus to a hurting world, unexpected circumstances to bring about holiness in His children, and an unexpectedly long timeline before Jesus returns. It's been more than two thousand years since Jesus promised He would come back and make all things new, but the promise hasn't been forgotten. Every part of your life, whether it's unexpected or not, serves the expected promise: Jesus' return and the restoration of all things.

Considerations

1. How is your life different from what you expected? (We tend to focus on the negative, but it can be better than you expected too!)

2. Are expectations always wrong? What are some examples of reasonable expectations?

3. What do you expect from God? How do you react when He doesn't allow things to play out the way you wanted?

A Little Bit Extra

A couple of years ago, we took a huge family trip to a theme park to celebrate some exciting milestones. We'd been to this park a handful of times and always left impressed by the staff and experience. Though we went during the "off" season, the park was incredibly crowded (likely due to intense winter storms across the country preventing people from leaving the area), and it was clear they hadn't anticipated this level of crowds. Bathrooms were dirty, attractions understaffed, and many employees tired and irritable, which was unlike our previous experiences. I began complaining about the conditions when someone I was with reminded me that the employees were doing as well as they could, and despite our expectations for a perfect vacation, we had to remember they were human beings trying their best to deal with a hard situation. It was a good reminder for me to always put people ahead of my expectations.

CHAPTER 12

The Contentment Conundrum

"Contentment is natural wealth, luxury is artificial poverty."

Socrates

If this is as good as life gets—if nothing ever changes—will it be enough?

I ask myself this question every so often, typically when I'm tired and standing in the TSA line at the airport waiting for my accordion to be flagged for extra screening. (They never know what to do with it or how to check it, so it could actually be my ticket to a life of crime.) No matter how good life is, so much of my effort is based on the hope of moving toward something better. But what if this is it? What if I never marry, never have my own family, never write a bestselling book, never have a viral comedy video, never put down roots? What if I pour out all my effort, try every door, pray every prayer, dream big and risk big, and have nothing to show for it? What if God says, "This is where

I have you, and this is where I want you to stay"? Will I be okay with that? Will I still be faithful?

Contentment* can be a finicky little beast. At the dictionary level, *contentment* is a state of happiness and satisfaction.[1] Contentment and expectations are frequently intertwined, as unmet expectations can quickly drive joy and peace out of our lives. Contentment can also be easily confused with apathy. Apathy happens when we believe things are as good as they can ever get, so we stop caring. Similar to cynicism, apathy says, "There's no point in even trying." Contentment, on the other hand, confidently shouts, "God, I know *You* are the point of all my efforts!"

Contentment isn't necessarily settling or denying ourselves nice things, exciting trips, or advancement in life. We're wired by God to pursue, provide, imagine, explore, advance, cultivate, discover, and dream. Contentment doesn't mean we ignore these elements of our personhood. It's the exact opposite, actually. Godly contentment is a hopeful tension between working *toward* what you want while being *completely satisfied* where you are. Contentment and ambition don't cancel each other out but rather go hand in hand. I can pursue my goals and dreams, but at the end of the day, I can rest confidently in God's plan, knowing He will only allow what's best for me to prosper.

---

* In writing this chapter, I've discovered I'm not content with the synonym options available in the English language for the word *contentment*. Most of them don't quite capture what I wish to convey in discussing the topic. So if you find yourself getting annoyed at my overuse of *contentment*, please know that I'm equally perturbed.

*Godly contentment is a hopeful tension between working **toward** what you want while being **completely satisfied** where you are.*

Chasing the Green

One of the most obvious areas in which we're meant to be satisfied is with our wealth and material possessions. At multiple points in Scripture, we're told to keep ourselves free from the love of money (1 Timothy 6:10; Hebrews 13:5, for examples). We're not told to keep ourselves free *from* money, only the *love* of it.

> And he said to them, "Take care, and be on your guard against all covetousness, for one's life does not consist in the abundance of his possessions." (Luke 12:15)

Money is necessary to survive and live, but if wealth or a certain type of lifestyle becomes your heart's main desire, you'll always be chasing greener pastures. Right now, you may be so bogged down by student loans and credit card debt that the idea of achieving any type of wealth seems laughable, but you can practice contentment even *before* you have a positive net worth. (If you're like me and don't know a lot of financial terms, a "positive net worth" means you have more money in your bank account than you owe. I heard the phrase on a podcast awhile back, and I try to drop it into a sentence every now and then to sound smart.) After all, if we can steward well when we have little, we'll be better prepared to steward well when we have a lot (Luke 16:10). Generosity and thankfulness start in our hearts, not when our bank accounts reach a certain number.

> But godliness with contentment is great gain, for we brought nothing into the world, and we cannot take anything out of the world. But if we have food and clothing, with these we will be content.
> (1 Timothy 6:6–8)

When Paul wrote this passage, he set the bar pretty low where material needs are concerned. Every time I see this verse I think, "*Only* food and clothes? That's really all I need to be content?" If I'm honest, I feel like I need so much more than those two things just to survive, much less flex my contentment muscles. What about housing? Security? Transportation? A working computer? I even feel like my phone is a legitimate need, as I'm not sure I could find my way out of my neighborhood without it. (I'm appropriately ashamed of that reality.) Perhaps I could justify it being part of my "clothes" since I don't feel fully dressed until it's in my pocket.

Our consumer-driven culture profits from convincing us that we require more than we actually need. It used to be you had to go window-shopping at a mall or find a JCPenney catalog to see everything you were missing out on, but now we see the latest and greatest continuously through our devices. All our searches, "likes," and purchases—and sometimes even our thoughts, it seems—are being tracked for marketing purposes and used to hit us with individual ads targeting our unique desires. We're constantly introduced to new products, programs, and subscriptions that promise us the next level of comfort, convenience, happiness, health, wealth, and fulfillment.

When Paul tells us to be satisfied with food and clothing, he's encouraging us to be glad for how God has provided for us right at this very moment. If we have food and clothing, then we can do God's will. If we can do God's will, then our life has purpose. And if we have purpose, we have a priceless treasure money could never buy!

> Keep falsehood and lies far from me: give me neither poverty nor riches, but give me only my daily bread. (Proverbs 30:8 NIV)

In Matthew 19:16, we're introduced to a wealthy young man who asked Jesus, "What good thing must I do to get eternal life?" (NIV).

Jesus told the young man to keep His commandments. Without missing a beat, the rich lad assured Jesus he had done just that.

> "All these I have kept," the young man said. "What do I still lack?"

> Jesus answered, "If you want to be perfect, go, sell your possessions and give to the poor, and you will have treasure in heaven. Then come, follow me."
>
> When the young man heard this, he went away sad, because he had great wealth. (vv. 20–22 NIV)

Today, wealth can be signified by organic diets, trendy gym memberships, exciting vacations, impressive Instagram posts, and having status with important people. Sometimes, those benefits of wealth are harder to give up than actual material possessions. In fact, the minimalism boom has made it popular to own as little as possible. When I felt God tugging on my heart to explore the idea of moving to South America to teach, it wasn't my "stuff" I was worried about leaving behind. I was concerned that I couldn't live without my access to vitamin supplements, health foods, and my yearly scuba-diving trips.

> Jesus said to them, "Truly I tell you, at the renewal of all things, when the Son of Man sits on his glorious throne, you who have followed me will also sit on twelve thrones, judging the twelve tribes of Israel. And everyone who has left houses or brothers or sisters or father or mother or wife or children or fields for my sake will receive a hundred times as much and will inherit eternal life. But many who are first will be last, and many who are last will be first." (Matthew 19:28–30 NIV)

We're meant to be content because nothing the world considers "wealth" is worth even a penny in God's economy. Wealth is like Monopoly money: it means something here on earth, but it's valueless in heaven. Many of us hold tightly to the fake currency our generation prioritizes when God offers us eternal riches in His kingdom. Fortunately, with God all things are possible (Matthew 19:26), including the ability to put our hope in eternal glory instead of earthly prosperity and security.

Having money brings both responsibility and opportunity to make choices that glorify God and impact the kingdom of heaven. The amount of money we make in life will vary greatly depending on our talents, skills, drive, God-given opportunities, and more. But with each dollar earned, we're given the chance to honor God with how we steward His resources.

Besides being the root of all kinds of evil (1 Timothy 6:10), the love of (or overdependence on) money can prevent us from living out the most important part of God's will: following Jesus. By viewing money through an eternal lens, though, we're freed to follow Jesus wherever He calls us to go.

Holy Discontentment

In my twenties, I was subtly taught that contentment was a prerequisite to receiving blessing. On more than one occasion, well-meaning men and women would say things to me like "Be joyful in your singleness, because that's when God will bring your husband!" *or* "Stop thinking about it and it will happen!"

Being satisfied with my life was presented as a way of getting what I ultimately wanted rather than a way of developing complete trust in my heavenly Father. Contentment, however, isn't something we use to "trick" God into giving us our desires. It provides us with the opportunity to place our own wills into His hands so we can grow and mature as believers.

> Strive for peace with everyone, and for the holiness without which no one will see the Lord. (Hebrews 12:14)

Because while we're meant to be content in our circumstances, we're never supposed to settle spiritually. In spiritual matters, we're meant to flee from sin and pursue, chase, and strive for holiness. In fact, the more discontent we are with our sinfulness, the easier contentment becomes in all other areas of life.

> For the love of money is a root of all kinds of evils. It is through this craving that some have wandered away from the faith and pierced themselves with many pangs.
> But as for you, O man of God, flee these things. Pursue righteousness, godliness, faith, love, steadfastness, gentleness. (1 Timothy 6:10–11)

While dissatisfaction with our wealth, circumstances, and status drives a wedge between us and the Lord, discontent with our sin drives us directly into the arms of our Savior, the only place where true satisfaction can be found.

Keep your life free from love of money, and be content with what you have, *for he has said, "I will never leave you nor forsake you."* (Hebrews 13:5, emphasis added)

We can be content in what we have for one reason only: our God, who loves us fiercely, will never leave or forsake us. Our employer may fire us or never promote us, the stock market may crash and take our savings with it, we may never have an Instagram-perfect marriage, but we can pursue, chase, and seek after the things of God with abandon.

Sometimes I'm okay with the idea of staying where I'm at until I take my last breath. Other times I look ten years into the future and imagine I'll go insane if nothing has changed. Realistically, none of us will be frozen exactly where we're at. Life changes whether we want it to or not. (And if we're being real, it feels like our circumstances change when we want them to stay the same, and then they stay the same when we want them to change.)

For the majority of my twenties, I only wanted to be where I wasn't. My calling, satisfaction, and joy were always somewhere in the future. Contentment allows us to see our calling in today and to experience joy right where we are.

Contentment allows us to see our calling in today and to experience joy right where we are.

I still catch myself grumbling about my circumstances some-times, but I've lived enough years and chased enough rabbits down holes (I've chased hundreds of metaphorical rabbits and one real one, but that's a story for another time) to know that all the tunnels lead right back to where I'm standing now. So perhaps I should look around and see what God has for me right here.

As I've learned more about God and seen His ongoing faithfulness in my life, contentment has become a steadier companion. Fulfillment doesn't have to wait until you get to the next big thing. True joy comes from understanding the character and nature of God and knowing that your life is part of a story much bigger than your own.

As you go through life, you'll probably experience seasons when peace comes easily and others when you struggle to embrace where God has you. We'll always be learning to balance satisfaction in God with our earthly desires. But as we journey toward contentment in our heavenly Father, here are a few things to keep in mind:

- *Contentment* believes God has me where I am for a reason and He's bringing me to where I'm sup-posed to be.
- *Contentment* trusts that God gave me talents and gifts for a reason, even if I wish I had more talent or giftings in different areas.
- *Contentment* understands that I work hard and steward my talents diligently but that God ordains advancement. (And yes, I can even be content and still humbly ask for a raise or promotion!)

- *Contentment* means wholly surrendering the outcome of my efforts to God.
- *Contentment* recognizes the incredible blessings God has already given me right where I'm standing.
- *Contentment* allows me to dream big and take responsible risks, because I know God will only give me success if it's what's best for me.

Embracing our circumstances frees us to live life with open hands, following what God has called us to do without the fear of losing everything. Because if we're always content, then we always have everything.

Considerations

1. In your own words, how would you describe contentment? In what area(s) of life are you desiring change but not getting anywhere?

2. When it comes to handling money, I've learned it helps to ask two questions: "Am I spending within my means?" and "Am I spending within God's heart?" How are you doing in those two areas?

3. Have you become too comfortable in your sin? How does being discontent in your sin drive you toward godly contentment? (Or do you even agree that it does?)

A Little Bit Extra

Deuteronomy 8:17–18 says this: "You may say to yourself, 'My power and the strength of my hands have produced this wealth for me.' But remember the LORD your God, for it is he who gives you the ability to produce wealth" (NIV). Money is a gift from God, and He should always be thanked for His provision. Gifts from God go counter to the fall and consequences of sin. Food, clothes, shelter, health, compatibility with others, wealth, victories, and success are all gifts granted by God despite the curse of sin. Turning these gifts into idols is wrong, but neither should we minimize the significance of the gifts God chooses to give us despite our sin. Pursuing gratitude helps us find the balance.

CHAPTER 13

Winning at Life

"Be genuine in all things. Life is a grand adventure!
The challenges, the people, and the searching and living
out our heart's desires culminate into one epic journey!
What would life be without adventure? Even more so,
what would adventure be without risk? And risk without
mystery? This fearful uncertainty requires great courage
to unveil, pursue, and make a reality. Have the courage
to do remarkable things! Whether grand or minuscule,
celebrated or obscure, pursue them with fervor because it is
with fervor that you will impact and change the world!"

Mark Weber (1988–2018)

Yesterday I had grand plans to complete this chapter. I'm three weeks out from my deadline to submit this manuscript to the publisher, and I've gone from "procrastination mode" to "anxious procrastination mode." (Anyone else have the spiritual gift of putting things off until the last minute?) Yesterday I set aside the whole evening to work on this book, but just before opening my computer to begin

writing, I went to get a jacket from my car and was surprised to find
it wet when I picked it up off the floorboard.

Well that's odd, I thought. *Did something spill?*

I checked under the seats to look for the source of liquid, only to
discover the floor of my car—both the front and back—completely
soaked. Not only was it soaked, but mold was already growing in the
carpets of my trusty Toyota Highlander.

"What the …" I stood, utterly flabbergasted. (I'd heard the word
flabbergasted used before, but only then did I personally understand
how it felt to *be* flabbergasted.)

The windows were rolled up. There weren't any bottles or con-
tainers that could've spilled. Somehow, my car had mysteriously
flooded. I had driven it less than twenty-four hours prior and hadn't
noticed a thing. When, and more importantly *how*, did this happen?

I didn't have much time to dwell on those trivial details, however, because the clock was now ticking. Not only did my scheduled
writing session need to be put on hold, but I was leaving the next
morning for a weekend of shows in California and wouldn't return
for four days. There was no way I could let this amount of water hang
out in my car that long. If it was already molding after a day, a whole
weekend unchecked would turn my car into a swamp.

Well this is poetic, I thought. *Adulting is going to keep me from
finishing my book about adulting.*

I started mopping up the water with towels, then placed a fan
toward the carpeting to help speed up the drying process (and to
blow all the mold spores into the air, making them easier for me to
inhale). After an hour I had still barely made a dent in the wetness.
My car was already really old and had been totaled a few years prior

in a hailstorm.* So I decided it wouldn't hurt anything just to cut out the carpets and throw them away to prevent further mold damage.

Finally, with the carpeting out of the equation and my car floor looking pathetic in its disrobement, I was able to dry up the water, finish packing, and go to bed around 2:00 a.m., crying on the inside as I set my alarm for 4:30 a.m.

I'm now sitting in the airport at my gate, and I just received an alert that my flight is delayed, putting me a little on edge about arriving on time for the show. I'm feeling the exhaustion of my late night and the stress of my car situation. I was hoping to get another year or two out of my current ride, but given its age and mileage, I figured that purchasing a decent used car might be the smartest and most economical option.

So I'm currently alternating between writing this chapter and shopping for used cars, trying to find something reliable that won't break the bank. I'm adulting on multiple levels, and despite my overall tiredness and bemused frustration at the timing of everything, I can't help but think that if this same scenario had happened a decade ago, it would've completely unraveled me. Panic, stress, and worry would've taken over, and I definitely would've called my parents by now in a meltdown. But here I am, handling everything like a champ. (Or maybe mold exposure has damaged the part of my brain that processes panic.)

I took a break from my adulting duties to text pictures of my torn-up car interior to my sister, captioning it "Look who's winning at life!"

---

* It was still drivable, so I kept it. The hail dents made it look like it had car-measles, which made it easier to find in crowded parking lots.

Winning at Life

Before Vine went the way of Myspace, my younger sister, Kathryn, sent me a video of a little girl standing on her front porch yelling "You're winning! You're winning at life!" to a man jogging by.

My sisters and I have adopted this phrase, and often say "You're winning at life!" to each other when we accomplish the most basic adulting tasks or sarcastically when we've clearly made a poor decision. Only recently, though, have I even felt remotely like I'm winning at life in a non-ironic sense.

When I first began adulting, I always wanted to know people's ages when they accomplished something big and hit a certain life milestone. I took extra comfort in stories where people were a bit older before they found their callings, got married, or achieved greatness.

They were called to the mission field at forty-five? Awesome!

They met their spouse at forty? I have a chance!

They didn't get their first writing contract until they were thirty-eight? Yes!

These stories gave me hope that I, too, might have a shot at those things, even if I didn't accomplish them all right away.

I had huge dreams and goals in my twenties. I wanted to author bestselling books, write for television, and travel the world. I wanted respect from my peers and to be noticed and praised by those I looked up to and admired. I wanted a circle of tight-knit friends, a husband to grow old with, and children to raise (and to guilt into living out all of my failed dreams).

I felt so much pressure to achieve, experience, and squeeze all I could out of life—and to do it quickly so that I could move on to the next thing and keep up with everyone else—that I didn't enjoy any part of it. I feared being stuck in the margins of ordinariness and ran hard to get to the "next level," even though I had no idea where these mythical "levels" were leading. Life felt like Candy Crush, where the programmers continuously added levels so I could never actually complete the game. I was living in an aimless rat race, and I was an anxious (and often melodramatic) bundle of misery and despair.

If I could go back in time, I'd tell twenty-five-year-old me: "Calm it down. I know it doesn't feel like it right now, but you're going to be okay."

And I'm going to say the same thing to you: It may not feel like it now, but you're going to be okay. You're going to be okay because you'll figure out how to find a dentist that takes your insurance. You're going to be okay because your job won't always be unfamiliar and intimidating. You're going to be okay because you'll learn that failure and rejection, though devastating in the moment, make you wiser and stronger. You're going to be okay because you'll realize life can be both very hard and very good at the same time. You're going to be okay because your dreams and desires will change in ways you can't imagine right now. But most of all, you're going to be okay because you serve a good God who loves you and will faithfully complete the work that He started in you (Philippians 1:6).

Adulting for Jesus

At the beginning of the book, I said that I wouldn't trade my life for anything. I stand by that statement, moldy swamp-car and everything. Had I known in my twenties that I'd be where I am today in my midthirties—still living with roommates, still unmarried, and still trying to figure out what I want to be when I grow up—I would've had anxiety insomnia for ten straight years.

Fortunately, God has made it so that our lives are revealed to us one day at a time instead of decades at a time. And though God's greatest desire is to see us trust Him and become more Christlike, He delights in His children (Psalm 18:19), and like any parent who delights in a child, God loves giving good gifts.

When I take a step back, I see that God *has* granted me many of my desires: deep and lasting friendships, a creatively fulfilling job, opportunities to pursue hobbies, a great church here in Atlanta, and the ability to travel and see the world. Had I gotten *everything* I wanted out of the last decade, though, I would have missed out on the biggest gift God has given me: peace in Him.

Your journey won't look like anyone else's, which is both immensely freeing and wildly terrifying. While I can't promise you that you'll get everything you want out of this life, I have this to offer you: joy in the Lord, and the ability to trust in the goodness of God's plan, is truly better than getting everything you want.

If joy in the Lord doesn't sound like the better end of the deal, take heart! (I'll say it again: God can handle our honesty.) Ten years ago, I saw God as a means to getting what I wanted out of life, not my life as a means to worshipping God. When pastors and spiritual leaders used to say "getting more of God" was the prize for obedience, I'd stare at them skeptically. I've learned that satisfaction in God alone is a concept that can be understood to a certain extent in your head, but it takes time, experience, and some spiritual wrestling to move to your heart.

If you're struggling to see God as enough, I want to encourage you to continue getting to know Him. Read the Bible with the intention of learning about your Creator and Father. Pray and ask your heavenly Father to show you His heart for the world and for your life. As you get to know God for who He is and not just for what He can give you, you'll gain a better understanding of who you are as His child. If you need a place to start, begin with Matthew, Mark, Luke, and John in the New Testament and get to know Jesus through His life here on earth. In becoming human, Jesus made an incomprehensible God accessible to us (Hebrews 4:15).

If you have a beating heart and breath in your lungs, then God is still moving and working in your life.

If you have a beating heart and breath in your lungs, then God is still moving and working in your life. So have hope and dream big, but do so openhandedly, allowing God to replace old, stagnating dreams with new, life-filled ones.

None of us knows what lies ahead. We know neither the trials, heartbreaks, or temptations awaiting us, nor the joys, gifts, and blessings lying around the corner. Fortunately, we serve a God who promises to sustain His children through anything. If you've repented of your sins and are following Jesus, then no matter what, you're winning at life.

Invisible Legacies

The quote at the very beginning of this chapter came from the writings of my younger brother, Mark, who was killed in action during a deployment to Iraq, as I shared before. After his death, something interesting happened. Hundreds of people reached out to our family with stories about how Mark had impacted their lives. For some, his goofy sense of humor and obsession with bizarre gifs brightened their days. For others, his passion for food—and the sheer volume of it he could consume—both amused them and gave them an appreciation for the simpler things in life. His words had a way of building people up, while his dedication to excellence in his work inspired others to apply themselves similarly. His eagerness to share the gospel led people to Jesus, and his constant quest to know more about God challenged fellow believers to grow.

Despite these stories, Mark died with no idea of the impact he had on those around him. Many of the things he was remembered for weren't big, life-changing actions or huge accomplishments. He is most remembered for being himself and pursuing Jesus.

Before Mark became a combat rescue officer with the special forces, he worked at a desk doing contracting for the Air Force. He felt like a failure, living a futile life trapped in a job he hated. He was in a near-constant state of depression and self-pity, until he had an encounter that changed his entire outlook on life.

On the way out of his building after working late one night, Mark happened upon a janitor mopping the hallways. The man was missing both arms up to his elbows and hugged the mop with his stubs. Rather than struggle with the task, the man sang and moved the mop up and down the floors in a dancing motion, turning the mundane job of cleaning linoleum into a little performance.

The sight of this man radiating so much joy in his circumstances triggered a drastic change in my brother's "woe is me" attitude. After that chance meeting, Mark turned his outlook on life from one of defeatism to one of gratefulness and joy. He began working out, got involved in his church and community, and explored the idea of changing to a more fulfilling career path. He started training to join the Air Force Pararescue team, a group of highly trained soldiers equipped to go into any situation and extract the injured, endangered, or deceased.

My brother's story and sacrifice have impacted and inspired many, but the janitor working that night will never know the role he played in my brother's life (unless he happens to stumble upon a list of "best-selling Christian books for millennials" online—thank you again for recommending this book to everyone you know). This man's legacy is woven into my brother's journey, though we'll likely never know his name.

In 2012 a band called The Script released a song called "Hall of Fame." The chorus of the song went like this (bonus points if you sing along as you read it):

Standing in the hall of fame
And the world's gonna know your name
'Cause you burn with the brightest flame
And the world's gonna know your name
And you'll be on the walls of the hall of fame[1]

Right now, in our influencer-obsessed culture, it's easy to confuse having a following with having an impact. People with large followings certainly can and do have an influence; but having a following isn't the same as having an impact, and being well-known isn't the same as being known.

Having a following isn't the same as having an impact, and being well-known isn't the same as being known.

One of the subtle lies feeding society right now is that your life only matters if your name is known and remembered. The truth, however, is that a hundred years from now most of us will be completely forgotten. (I just wanted to saturate you in my spiritual gift of encouragement before ending this book.) Even if your name is eventually forgotten, though, your legacy will continue.

Perhaps you've heard of the "butterfly effect," the concept of one simple action triggering large changes elsewhere. While alive, most of us will have no idea of the impact we're having on those around us. The smile to a stranger, word of encouragement to someone at your job, or prayer you offer for a friend in a time of need could have eternal implications invisible to the naked eye. We don't always know the effects our choices have on others, what seeds take root, or how far the ripples reach once the stone of endeavor is cast into the pond of life.

> For we are his workmanship, created in Christ Jesus
> for good works, which God prepared beforehand,
> that we should walk in them. (Ephesians 2:10)

God has prepared good works for us to do in advance, and by living for Jesus, we'll naturally step into these good works as our personality, talents, and even our weaknesses and struggles impact and encourage others.

This legacy of good works, though, will be largely invisible to us and may even be invisible to most of the world. We don't see the sun half of the time, but we know it's there. Just because we don't see the purpose in every little thing doesn't mean purpose is absent. Either it hasn't been revealed to us yet or God has chosen to keep it hidden.

> Better is a handful of quietness than two hands full
> of toil and a striving after wind. (Ecclesiastes 4:6)

My prayer as you finish this book and begin adulting with new purpose is that you'll find quietness in the middle of our noisy, rapidly changing, distraction-filled world. I hope you won't feel the need to constantly toil and strive for meaning and worth, but that God will give you a peaceful confidence that every part of your life—even the things you'd rather change—was given to you intentionally and for a purpose.

The pressure to do it all, have it all, be it all, feel it all, and experience it all will crush you. Place the burden to adult perfectly on Jesus. It's a weight too strong for you to carry.

When we get to heaven, God isn't going to ask if we had good self-esteem, achieved everything on our bucket lists, or felt constantly fulfilled.

He's going to see the blood of Jesus, smile, and say, "Well done, my good and faithful servant." You'll see that your name, though it may be forgotten on earth, has been written in God's book of life since the founding of the world (Revelation 3:5; 17:8).

Then, once in the kingdom of God, where sin, pain, and struggle are forever removed, you will finally get to see how God weaved your adulting into the grand story of redemption and eternity.

Considerations

1. What legacy do you think your life is leaving? In what ways might your legacy continue through eternity?

2. How well do you know God? What do you know about Him?
What would you like to learn?

3. Do you feel like you're winning at life? Why, or why not?

A Little Bit Extra

Since I left you hanging about my vehicle situation: After returning from my trip to California, I managed to find a great deal on a low-mileage, used Toyota Camry. The dealer even let me trade in my hail-damaged, water-logged Highlander for a little cash toward the purchase. It was my first time negotiating and purchasing a vehicle by myself, and I finally feel qualified to have written a book on adulting. Selah.

Author Note

I'm not sure how familiar you are with "traditional" book publishing, but from the time a book proposal is picked up by a publishing house to the time it is actually released can be a long time. In the case of *Adulting for Jesus*, I began writing the proposal in the summer of 2019, a contract was signed with David C Cook publishing in December of that year, and I did most of the actual writing in January to March of 2020.

I alluded to it a few times in the book, but in the week leading up to my deadline, the COVID-19 pandemic shut down the United States and most of the world. Right now, I am out of work for the foreseeable future, and I'm so unsure of when "normal" might return that I'm looking for jobs at grocery stores and online delivery services to get me through until this "plague" runs its course. I'm sure you experienced this uncertainty and made life adjustments as well.

Here's the strange part to me: This book has a February 2021 release date, so by the time you read it, life might be back to normal. Or perhaps we'll have divided into factions and be fighting in our own version of Hunger Games. (Oh, what I wouldn't give for a time machine so I know whether to start training!)

This pandemic revealed raw insight into what real adulting looks like: it is completely unpredictable, and security in anything outside of God is an illusion.

At the suggestion of many authors I respect, I most likely won't be reading online reviews for this book. Please feel free to be honest in your feedback in order to help others determine whether it might be a good fit for their libraries, but if you have any comments, questions, or Chipotle hacks for me directly, send them to: Kristintriedherbest@gmail.com.

I welcome your thoughts, good or bad, but please bear in mind that (a) I am human; and (b) though I've developed pretty thick skin from years of open mics and volunteering in middle school ministry, I still have feelings. We used to wrap my dog's heartworm pills in meat to help him take them. If you feel the need to rip me to shreds, please do it with the language equivalent of filet mignon.

Thank you again for reading my book, and I hope to meet you someday in person (assuming social distancing hasn't become a permanent thing).

Sincerely,
Kristin Weber

Additional Reading

Want some additional reading ideas about life, adulting, and growth? I recommend these books:

Atomic Habits: Tiny Changes, Remarkable Results by James Clear (Avery, 2018)

Boundaries: When to Say Yes, How to Say No, to Take Control of Your Life by Dr. Henry Cloud and Dr. John Townsend (Zondervan, 2017)

Don't Waste Your Life by John Piper (Crossway, 2003)

Garden City: Work, Rest, and the Art of Being Human by John Mark Comer (Zondervan, 2015)

Get a Financial Life by Beth Kobliner (Simon & Schuster, updated 2019)

The Gospel at Work: How the Gospel Gives New Purpose and Meaning to Our Jobs by Sebastian Traeger and Greg Gilbert (Zondervan, 2018)

Just Do Something: A Liberating Approach to Finding God's Will by Kevin DeYoung (Moody, 2014)

Messy Beautiful Friendship: Finding and Nurturing Deep and Lasting Relationships by Christine Hoover (Baker Books, 2017)

A Small Book for the Anxious Heart by Edward T. Welch (New Growth Press, 2019)

12 Ways Your Phone Is Changing You by Tony Reinke (Crossway, 2017)

Winning the Worry Battle by Barb Roose (Abingdon Press, 2018)

Notes

Chapter 1: Chasing Unicorns, Callings, and Perfect Decisions

1. Sam Allberry, "Why God Hides His Will for You" *Desiring God*, July 2, 2019, www.desiringgod.org/articles/why-god-hides-his-will-for-you.

Chapter 2: The Struggle Is Too Real

1. "Augusta Louise (1753–1835)" in "Noblewomen and the Bible: Seven Stories from the House of Stolberg," Museum of the Bible, accessed August 27, 2020, www.museumofthebible.org/exhibits/noblewomen-and-the-bible.

2. Richard W. Rahn, "Common Folk Live Better Now Than Royalty Did in Earlier Times," *Washington Times*, December 22, 2014, www.washingtontimes.com/news /2014/dec/22/richard-rahn-loux-xiv-john-rockefeller-had-harder-/.

3. "Inside Quest: Millennials in the Workplace," video interview with Simon Sinek. Full interview can be viewed here: www.youtube.com/watch?v=hER0Qp6QJNU.

4. Maura Thomas, "How to Overcome Your (Checks Email) Distraction Habit," *Harvard Business Review*, December 4, 2019, https://hbr.org/2019/12/how-to -overcome-your-checks-email-distraction-habit.

5. Lindsay Dodgson, "Why You Find It Hard to Pick Your Lunch or a Netflix Show, according to New Research," *Business Insider*, October 4, 2018, www.businessinsider .com/why-too-much-choice-is-bad-2018-10.

Chapter 3: Fading Glory

1. The whole creation and fall account can be found in the first several chapters of Genesis.

2. "40 Quotes about Life (for a Pessimist)," *Telegraph*, accessed August 17, 2020, www.telegraph.co.uk/books/what-to-read/40-quotes-about-life-for-a-pessimist/jim -carrey-/. See also "Jim Carrey's Commencement Address at the 2014 MUM Graduation," speech video (esp. 19:12), May 30, 2014, www.youtube.com/watch ?v=V80-gPkpH6M.

3. Paul David Tripp, "The Call for Holiness in Light of the Second Coming," speech video (esp. 20:00), February 10, 2020, https://bcsmn.edu/archive-video/the-call-for-holiness-in-the-light-of-the-second-coming/.

Chapter 4: Work: It Does a Soul Good

1. "Retirement Blues: Taking It Too Easy Can Be Hard on You," Harvard Health Publishing, accessed August 18, 2020, www.health.harvard.edu/mens-health/retirement-stress-taking-it-too-easy-can-be-bad-for-you.

2. Gene Edward Veith, "Which Vocations Should Be Off Limits to Christians?," Gospel Coalition, March 22, 2012, www.thegospelcoalition.org/article/which-vocations-should-be-off-limits-to-christians.

3. Full credit for the word *jobby* goes to Tyra Banks.

Chapter 6: I Can Do All the Things

1. "Par for the course" is a phrase that commoners like me have stolen from golf as a fancy way of saying "what's expected."

2. Story used with permission. For more information on Johnnie and his speaking, visit www.johnnieyellock.com.

3. Aaron Menikoff, "Be Tender-Hearted and Thick-Skinned: How Humility Protects Pastors from Pastoral Burnout," 9Marks, July 17, 2018, www.9marks.org/article/be-tender-hearted-and-thick-skinned-how-humility-protects-pastors-from-pastoral-burnout/.

4. William McRaven, "If You Want to Change the World, Start Off by Making Your Bed," speech video, August 17, 2017, www.youtube.com/watch?v=3sK3wJAxGfs&t=70s.

Chapter 7: Finding Rest in an Anti-Sabbath World

1. Megan U. Boyanton, "Burnout Is a Medical Condition. Why Do So Many of Us Millennials Suffer from It?," *Republic*, June 26, 2019, www.azcentral.com/story/opinion/op-ed/2019/06/26/millennial-burnout-real-why-so-many-feel/1527877001/.

2. Sinclair Ferguson, "Sabbath Rest," *Tabletalk Magazine*, March 1, 2004, Ligonier Ministries, www.ligonier.org/learn/articles/sabbath-rest/.

Chapter 8: The Social Media Monster

1. Leanna Garfield, "Checking Your Phone First Thing in the Morning Could Be Making You Unhappy," *Business Insider*, May 25, 2016, www.businessinsider.com/why-you-shouldnt-check-your-phone-first-thing-in-the-morning-2016-5.

2. Stassi Reid, "12 Things NOT to Do in Bolivia," *Destination Tips*, June 12, 2017, www.destinationtips.com/destinations/south-america/12-things-not-bolivia/12/.

3. Jacquelle Crowe, "Unplug, iGen: Put the Phone Down and Live," *Desiring God*, July 10, 2018, www.desiringgod.org/articles/unplug-igen.

4. Shannon Brake and AsapSCIENCE, "5 Ways Social Media Is Changing Your Brain," video, TED-Ed, accessed August 18, 2020, https://ed.ted.com/featured /qQzsdX2Y#watch.

5. Trevor Haynes, "Dopamine, Smartphones, and You: A Battle for Your Time," Harvard University (blog), May 1, 2018, http://sitn.hms.harvard.edu/flash/2018 /dopamine-smartphones-battle-time/.

6. Kelly McSweeney, "This Is Your Brain on Instagram: Effects of Social Media on the Brain," *Now*, March 17, 2019, https://now.northropgrumman.com/this-is -your-brain-on-instagram-effects-of-social-media-on-the-brain.

7. Mattha Busby, "Social Media Copies Gambling Methods to Create Psychological Cravings," *Guardian*, May 8, 2018, www.theguardian.com/technology/2018/may /08/social-media-copies-gambling-methods-to-create-psychological-cravings.

8. Arlene Pellicane, *Calm, Cool, and Connected: 5 Digital Habits for a More Balanced Life* (Chicago: Moody, 2017), 90.

9. From a talk titled "It Is Well with My Phone." Used with permission from Arlene Pellicane.

Chapter 9: Friendship Is the Best Ship

1. Neil Howe, "Millennials and the Loneliness Epidemic," *Forbes*, May 3, 2019, www.forbes.com/sites/neilhowe/2019/05/03/millennials-and-the-loneliness -epidemic/#2f0a73237676.

2. Ellie Polack, "New Cigna Study Reveals Loneliness at Epidemic Levels in America," Cigna, May 1, 2018, www.cigna.com/newsroom/news-releases/2018 /new-cigna-study-reveals-loneliness-at-epidemic-levels-in-america.

3. Lale Arikoglu, "How I Learned to Love Dining Alone: Feeling Adrift in New York after a Transatlantic Move, Eating Alone Helped Me Get to Know the City— and Myself," *Condé Nast Traveler*, January 31, 2019, www.cntraveler.com/story /how-i-learned-to-love-dining-alone.

4. Social distancing and masks don't make things any easier, either. Hopefully that will all be behind us by the time you read this book.

5. Tony Reinke, *12 Ways Your Phone Is Changing You* (Wheaton, IL: Crossway, 2017), 70.

6. Albert Jack, *Shaggy Dogs and Black Sheep: The Origins of Even More Phrases We Use Every Day* (New York: Penguin, 2005), loc. 1218 of 3125, Kindle.

7. Andrew Marin, "Transparency and Vulnerability," Patheos (blog), September 4, 2013, www.patheos.com/blogs/loveisanorientation/2013/09/transparency-and -vulnerability/.

Chapter 10: Cue the Anxiety

1. Lila MacLellan, "Millennials Experience Work-Disrupting Anxiety at Twice the Average US Rate," Quartz, December 5, 2018, https://qz.com/work/1483697 /millennials-experience-work-disrupting-anxiety-at-twice-the-us-average-rate/.

2. Associated Press, "College Students Turn to 'Adulting' Classes for Basic Life Skills," Fox Business, November 2018, www.foxbusiness.com/money/college -students-turn-to-adulting-classes-for-basic-life-skills.

3. Beth Moore, "Esther: It's Tough Being a Woman" speech video (esp. 40:00), session 3, *The Faithful: Heroes of the Old Testament*, LifeWay.

Chapter 11: Operation Expectation Adjustment

1. Alison Bonds Shapiro, "Being Wary of Our Expectations," *Psychology Today*, October 4, 2012, www.psychologytoday.com/us/blog/healing-possibility/201210 /being-wary-our-expectations.

2. Margarita Tartakovsky, "How to Relinquish Unrealistic Expectations," Psych Central, October 8, 2018, https://psychcentral.com/lib/how-to-relinquish -unrealistic-expectations/.

3. "What Does It Mean for Jesus to Be Your True North?," Got Questions, accessed August 18, 2020, www.gotquestions.org/Jesus-true-north.html.

4. The story of Abraham and Sarah is found in Genesis 12–25.

5. United Church of God, "The Messiah's Misunderstood Mission," Beyond Today, January 26, 2011, www.ucg.org/bible-study-tools/booklets/jesus-christ-the -real-story/the-messiahs-misunderstood-mission.

Chapter 12: The Contentment Conundrum

1. *Oxford US Dictionary*, s.v. "contentment," Lexico, accessed August 18, 2020, www.lexico.com/en/definition/contentment.

Chapter 13: Winning at Life

1. "Hall of Fame," featuring will.i.am, track 3 on The Script, *#3*, Sony Music Entertainment UK, 2012.